Seventeen Years in Alaska

RASMUSON LIBRARY HISTORICAL TRANSLATION SERIES

Marvin W. Falk, Series Editor

The Rasmuson Library Historical Translation Series makes accessible translations of works of historical importance on the Circumpolar North available to English-speaking readers.

Titles in the Series

Volume 1. *Holmberg's Ethnographic Sketches by Heinrich Johan Holmberg.* Edited by Marvin W. Falk; translated by Fritz Jaensch, 1985.

Volume 2. *Tlingit Indians of Alaska by Anatolii Kamenskii.* Translated and introduction by Sergei Kan, 1985.

Volume 3. *Bering's Voyages: The Reports from Russia.* By Gerhard Friedrich Müller, translated with commentary by Carol Urness, 1986.

Volume 4. *Russian Exploration in Southwest Alaska: The Travel Journals of Petr Korsakovskiy (1818) and Ivan Ya. Vasilev (1829).* Edited and introduction by James VanStone; translated by David H. Kraus, 1988.

Volume 5. *The Khlebnikov Archive: Unpublished Journal (1800–1837) and Travel Notes (1820, 1822, and 1824).* Edited by Leonid Shur; translated by John Bisk, 1990.

Volume 6. *The Great Russian Navigator, A. I. Chirikov.* By Vasilii A. Divin, translated and annotated by Raymond H. Fisher, 1993.

Volume 7. *Journals of the Priest Ioann Veniaminov in Alaska, 1923 to 1836.* Introduction and commentary by S. A. Mousalimas; translated by Jerome Kisslinger, 1993.

Volume 8. *To the Chukchi Peninsula and the Tlingit Indians 1881/1882: Journals and Letters by Aurel and Arthur Krause.* Translated by Margot Krause McCaffrey, 1993.

Volume 9. *Essays on the Ethnography of Aleuts.* By R. G. Liapunova, translated by Jerry Shelest with W. B. Workman and Lydia T. Black, 1996.

Volume 10. *Fedor Petrovich Litke* by A. I. Alekseev. Edited by Katherine L. Arndt; translated by Serge LeComte, 1996.

Volume 11. *Grewingk's Geology of Alaska and the Northwest Coast of America: Contributions toward Knowledge of the Orographic and Geognostic Condition of the North-West Coast of America, with the Adjacent Islands.* By Constantine Grewingk, edited by Marvin W. Falk; translated by Fritz Jaensch, 2003.

Volume 12. *Steller's History of Kamshatka: Collected Information Concerning the History of Kamshatka, Its Peoples, Their Manners, Names, Lifestyle, and Various Customary Practices.* By George Steller, translated by Margritt Engel and Karen Willmore, 2003.

Volume 13. *Through Orthodox Eyes: Russian Missionary Narratives of Travels to the Dena'ina and Ahtna, 1850s–1930s.* Edited and introduction by Andrei A. Znamenski, 2003.

Volume 14. *Until Death Do Us Part: The Letters and Travels of Anna and Vitus Bering.* By Peter Ulf Møller and Natasha Okhotina Lind, translated by Anna Halager, 2009.

Volume 15. *Natalia Shelikhova: Russian Oligarch of Alaska Commerce.* Edited and translated by Dawn Lea Black and Alexander Yu. Petrov, 2010.

Volume 16. *Seventeen Years in Alaska: A Depiction of Life Among the Indians of Yakutat.* By Albin Johnson, edited and translated by Mary Ehrlander, 2014.

Seventeen Years in Alaska

A Depiction of Life Among the Indians of Yakutat

Albin Johnson

posted by the Swedish Mission Organization, 1889

Edited and Translated by

Mary Ehrlander

University of Alaska Press
Fairbanks, Alaska

University of Alaska Press
P.O. Box 756240
Fairbanks, AK 99775-6240

Library of Congress Cataloging-in-Publication Data

Johnson, Albin, 1865–1947.
[Sjutton ar i Alaska. English]
Seventeen years in Alaska : a depiction of life among the Indians of Yakutat / by Albin Johnson, posted by the Swedish Mission's Organization, 1889 ; translated by Mary Ehrlander.
pages cm. — (Rasmuson library historical translation series ; v. 16)
Includes index.
Translation of: Sjutton ar i Alaska.
ISBN 978-1-60223-211-2 (pbk. : alk. paper)—ISBN 978-1-60223-212-9 (electronic)
1. Tlingit Indians—Missions—Alaska—Yakutat Bay Region. 2. Tlingit Indians—Alaska—Yakutat Bay Region—Social life and customs. 3. Johnson, Albin, 1865-1947—Travel--Alaska—Yakutat Bay Region. 4. Missionaries—Alaska—Yakutat Bay Region—Biography. 5. Missionaries—Sweden—Biography. 6. Svenska missionsförbundet—History. I. Ehrlander, Mary, translator. II. Title.
E99.T6J6413 2014
979.8004'9727—dc23

2013014107

Cover illustration: Natives, Yakutat, Alaska. Alaska State Library, Edward DeGroff Collection. Photographs, ca. 1886–1890. ASL-PCA-91.

This publication was printed on acid-free paper that meets the minimum requirements for ANSI / NISO Z39.48–1992 (R2002) (Permanence of Paper for Printed Library Materials).

Printed in the United States

Contents

Introduction

The Swedish Evangelical Mission Covenant in America has played important roles in shaping Alaska's history through its efforts not only in spreading the gospel but also in advancing education; providing medical care to Alaska Natives; introducing alternative food sources, including vegetable gardens and domesticated reindeer; shielding the Native population from the harmful influences of Western culture; and generally advocating for the Native peoples of Alaska. Implicit in all of these endeavors was the goal of "civilizing" the Natives, a pursuit in which the government and missionaries worked hand in hand. Missionaries of numerous denominations profoundly influenced the experiences of thousands of Alaska Natives in the late nineteenth and early twentieth centuries. With the translation of missionary Albin Johnson's account of his seventeen years among the Tlingit of Yakutat from 1889 to 1907, Alaska history enthusiasts will have access to a valuable perspective on conditions in Alaska not long after Alaska's purchase from Russia in 1867, when the region and its Native peoples were being overrun by migrants, most of whom sought economic opportunity and felt little or no commitment to the territory or its people. Commercial fisheries and individual migrants were depleting the Natives' subsistence resources. With astonishing speed, technological advancement and economic development were ending the isolation and relative tranquility of some of the more remote communities, such as Yakutat, and casting Alaska Natives into the twentieth century with little preparation. The allure of wage labor opportunities and of Western commodities, including liquor, were irresistible and would bring destabilizing and irreversible change. As Johnson's memoir demonstrates, missionaries sought to mitigate the negative effects of these Western influences, and they contributed to the well-being of Alaska Natives in myriad ways, while at the same time engendering profound change themselves. Johnson's anecdote about the children's belief that the Bible and the Montgomery Ward catalogue were the most read books in the world aptly illustrated the powerful impacts of these Western forces.

MISSIONARY MEMOIRS AS PRIMARY SOURCES ON ALASKA HISTORY

This translation complements volumes 2 and 13 in the Rasmuson Historical Translation Series, which provide Russian Orthodox perspectives of encounters with Tlingit and with Dena'ina and Ahtna, respectively, both of which accounts are generally contemporary with Albin Johnson's experience at Yakutat. Sergei Kan's translation of Fr. Anatolii Kamenskii's *Tlingit Indians of Alaska,* a Tlingit ethnography, is based on Kamenskii's years as Sitka's parish priest from 1895 to 1898. Kamenskii's book is much more strictly ethnographical than Johnson's memoir. However, Kan included other documents in the translation that reveal more explicitly Kamenskii's attitudes toward Tlingit life ways, as well as his efforts to fight alcohol abuse and other pathological behaviors and his battles with the Presbyterians, with whom the Orthodox competed in Sitka. Unlike Johnson and other Covenant missionaries who enjoyed a good relationship with General Education Agent and Presbyterian missionary Sheldon Jackson, Kamenskii sharply criticized Jackson's oversight of Native education. Labeling Jackson "unfit for the task," Kamenskii called for much greater authority for teachers, such as that exerted by Episcopal Father William Duncan over the Tsimshian of Metlakatla. "Some kind of guardianship" was essential until the Indians developed "an independent civilized life," Kamenskii declared.[1] Kamenskii and Johnson exhibited similar paternalistic and ethnocentric attitudes toward the Tlingit. Both clearly were dedicated to the well-being of the Tlingit, but they wrote of them at times as if they were children, while expressing their confidence that the Tlingit had great potential for becoming civilized.

Through Orthodox Eyes: Russian Missionary Narratives of Travels to the Dena'ina and Ahtna, 1850s–1930s, translated and with an introduction by Andrei A. Znamenski, extends well before and after Johnson's *Seventeen Years in Alaska*. In contrast to Johnson's memoir and Kamenskii's ethnography, *Through Orthodox Eyes* includes the narratives of numerous Russian Orthodox clergy, most of whom traveled extensively to serve the Dena'ina and Ahtna in the far-flung villages of their regions. The clergy sometimes came into contact with their "flocks" only once every few years, whereas Kamenskii and Johnson lived among the Tlingit in Sitka and Yakutat, respectively. Inland Dena'ina and Ahtna communities were remote and not easily accessible; thus struggles against the natural environment dominate the clerics' journals. As Znamenski wrote in his introduction to *Through Orthodox Eyes*, the Orthodox clergy's greatest foe was not Native "ignorance" but "arctic elements."[2]

Carrie M. Willard Among the Tlingits: The Letters of 1881–1883 offers yet another missionary perspective of encounters between missionaries, in this case Presbyterian, and the Tlingit in the 1880s. At the request of Chilkat people in the region, she and her husband, Eugene Willard, established a mission on Portage Bay; they named the settlement Haines.[3] The Willards arrived at a time of great internecine "troubles," which, according to Willard, the missionaries helped the Chilkats to resolve. Like other missionary letters and memoirs, Willard's letters relate the missionaries' determined efforts to relieve the Tlingit's suffering from dreadful diseases. Epidemics threatened the Tlingit's lives, endangering the race and culture, while at the same time pitting the missionaries' spiritual and medical credibility against that of shamans. A strength of Willard's writing is its treatment of the deep dilemmas that Natives faced as they considered the validity of Western and Christian versus traditional beliefs. The consequences of their decisions, after all, were potentially great.

Other turn-of-the-century Alaska missionary memoirs include that of John Wight Chapman, Episcopal missionary at the Athabaskan village of Anvik, at the confluence of the Anvik and Yukon rivers, from 1887 to 1930. When Chapman arrived, the Ten'ah "had hardly emerged from the Stone Age"; they had been exposed to a few trade items and knew a bit of Russian, which was used in trade, but English "was wholly unknown."[4] The Indians of Anvik lived in partially subterranean dwellings when Chapman arrived, and they wore fish-skin clothing in the summer and fur clothing in the winter; a few owned shotguns, which they used for hunting large animals, but they used bows and bone-tipped arrows to hunt small game. They made fish traps from local materials. The description of initial struggles with communication followed by Chapman learning the Native language and the Indians learning English is one of the richest features of *A Camp on the Yukon*. Like Johnson's, Chapman's memoir contains short chapters that illustrate myriad traditional beliefs, practices, and taboos of the indigenous people before and as rapid change occurred owing to in-migration of non-Natives.

Episcopal Archbishop Hudson Stuck's memoir *Ten Thousand Miles With a Dog Sled* is a good source on conditions among the Athabaskans of the Interior in the early 1900s. Like the Russian Orthodox clerics in the Dena'ina and Ahtna regions of Southcentral Alaska, Stuck traveled widely to visit the villages in the broad expanse of Alaska's Interior. Stuck explicitly opposed assimilation of Natives, though of course he aimed to Christianize them. He expressed appreciation of Native languages and reported his preference for teaching and preaching in the Native tongues, though this was not always possible. He repeatedly noted his approval of translation of the Bible into Native languages. Unlike many other missionaries, Stuck described Native dancing as completely inoffensive and innocent, although he expressed revulsion for the medicine men, whom he said threatened and abused the people.[5] Another distinctive, though certainly not unique, characteristic of Stuck's memoir was his repeated condemnations of the "low down white men" who exploited Natives by selling them liquor and/or seducing Native women.

In *The Yup'ik Eskimos,* ethnologist Ann Fienup-Riordan compiled, annotated, and contextualized the journals, letters, and ethnographic accounts of John and Edith Kilbuck, Moravian missionaries in Bethel from 1886 to 1900. The extensive journals the two kept were actually accounts of daily activities and reflections that they wrote *to one another* during John Kilbuck's long absences from the mission as he traveled throughout southwest Alaska to proselytize and acquaint himself with the people. Kilbuck's keen observation skills, along with his empathy for the people, allowed him to produce remarkably insightful renderings of the Yup'ik people and their way of life. According to Fienup-Riordan, "scholars who know the material agree that John Henry Kilbuck's observations are among the most perceptive and most accurate of any of the early missionaries working in the area."[6] The Kilbucks, like other missionaries, sought to introduce a new way of life to the Yup'ik as they worked not only to Christianize and "civilize" them but also to educate them according to Western standards, thereby eradicating heathen practices and habits. Nevertheless, the Kilbucks clearly appreciated the Yup'ik culture and people, perhaps owing partially to John's own Delaware Indian heritage. The Kilbucks and their fellow missionaries immediately set to work learning the Native language, knowing that communication would be essential to attaining their other goals.

The journals of Moravian missionary Ella Mae Romig, edited by Phyllis Movius in *When the Geese Come*, complement the Kilbucks' journals. Romig and her husband, Dr. Joseph Herman Romig, spent nine years among the Yup'ik at the Moravian mission in Bethel from 1896 to 1903 and at the Carmel Mission at the mouth of the Nushagak River from 1904 to 1905. Owing to epidemic diseases that were devastating the Yup'ik people in the region, the Moravian Church sent the Romigs to Bethel to provide medical care to the Yup'ik as well as to assist in the mission's other endeavors. Ella Romig's candid reflections capture missionary attitudes toward Natives, tensions among the Moravian missionaries, competition with other missions in the region, and missionaries' concerns as wage labor opportunities, increasing materialism, and Western vices lured Natives from mission and Christian values.

Apaurak in Alaska: Social Pioneering Among the Eskimos, based on the journals and other writings of Norwegian Lutheran missionary T. L. Brevig, provides documentation of the traditional ways of the Iñupiat as they experienced rapid sociocultural and economic change at the turn of the twentieth century. Brevig was sent to Alaska's Seward Peninsula in 1894 to pastor Norwegian Sami, who had been brought there under Sheldon Jackson's plan to supplement the Native food supply and civilize the Eskimo of the region through the domestication of reindeer. Brevig managed the reindeer station at Teller for many years while Swedish Covenant missions on the Seward Peninsula also were engaged in the reindeer domestication project. Among other episodes, Brevig's journals, translated and edited by J. Walter Johnshoy, recorded the devastating effects of epidemics, in particular the 1900 measles and influenza epidemic that decimated Native villages on the Seward Peninsula, and the dedication of mission personnel in aiding the ill. So many children were orphaned in 1900 that Brevig established an orphanage at a location that came to be called Brevig Mission.[7] Passages related to language acquisition by both the Brevigs and the Natives, as well as his descriptions of the Natives' inquisitiveness regarding spiritual matters, are particularly insightful. The Brevigs' experience exemplified that of missionaries who became acculturated to the indigenous way of life; indeed the Iñupiat, in a ceremony, pronounced the Reverend and Mrs. Brevig Eskimos and named him *Apaurak*, the Father of All.

Sister Mary Joseph Calasanctius' *The Voice of Alaska: A Missioner's Memories* relates the experiences of this Flemish member of the Catholic order the Sisters of Saint Ann, which founded the mission at Holy Cross on the lower Yukon River in 1888. She served at Holy Cross until 1905; thus her memoirs, published first in 1929, cover the same time span as Johnson's service in Yakutat. The demographics at Holy Cross differed from those of the other mission stations treated here in that while it was in Ten'ah Athabaskan territory, the mission boarding and day school also served Eskimo and a few white children. The Catholic fathers canvassed the region looking for orphans and other children to attend the mission boarding school; in 1891 the mission school housed eighty Eskimo and Ten'ah students, and with the day-school children from nearby Koserefsky, enrollment was well above one hundred students. The missionaries hoped that the children, who during several years at the boarding school adopted Western and Christian values and traits, would return to their home villages and serve as role models, thus multiplying the impact of the mission work. In contrast to many other missionaries, including Johnson and other Covenant pastors, Sister Mary Joseph was rather tolerant of Native traditional practices such as the potlatch. She described the potlatch as a "feast for the exchange of goods" and described the dancing with masks with no hint of disapproval. Naturally she was not fully appreciative of the Ten'ah's religious beliefs and "nonsensical traditions," and she saw no good in the shamans. Theirs was a "real service of the devil... as those Shamans who have been converted attest," she wrote. "The very souls of the people are enchained by his tyranny."[8] On the other hand, Sister Mary Joseph described with good humor an incident during which she inadvertently interrupted a stick dance ceremony, which led a shaman to scream at her "something to the effect that I was an audacious rat to have interrupted their ceremony." Having conveyed through sign language her apologies, she quickly exited.[9]

Albin Johnson's memoirs, like these other missionary journals and memoirs, reflected outsiders' perceptions of Alaska Native cultures at a time when they were being inundated by myriad foreign influences. All describe Alaska Native cultures in transition through the eyes, assumptions, and values of "foreigners" who clearly felt concern and affection for the indigenous peoples and admired much about their character and skills. The missionaries all sought to protect Alaska Natives from harmful Western influences. At the same time, all also envisioned a positive future for these peoples not only in adopting Christian beliefs and values but also in acculturation, if not assimilation, with Western culture.

These missionaries generally expressed disapprobation of shamanistic beliefs and practices and concern about the anxiety and fear that shamans instilled in the people. However, the missionaries' responses to other traditional and spiritual beliefs varied, from interest and acceptance, as expressed by Sister Mary Joseph and Hudson Stuck, to sharp rejection, for instance by the Covenanters in the case of the potlatch. They believed that the ceremony exhibited the darkest hedonism and social pathology, owing to alcohol consumption at the feasts and the concern that diseases, particularly tuberculosis, spread during these festivities because of the numbers of people crowded into the potlatch venues. Learning from these primary sources the missionaries' concerns regarding traditional practices helps the scholar to understand, if not approve of, some of the missionaries' energetic efforts to uproot them.

These memoirs and journals also reveal the ways in which the preaching, teaching, and healing roles of the missionaries intertwined and how the material, health, and prestige benefits of association with missionaries contributed to conversion rates. The Natives' need for medical care drew them to the missionaries, and the effectiveness of Western medical care, limited as it was, clearly evoked gratitude in the Natives and lent credibility to the missionaries' words and practices in general. All of these works manifest the missionaries' deep devotion to their flocks, their relentless efforts to help Alaska Natives in their suffering, and their despair at the enormous death toll from diseases. These sources also illustrate that Natives recognized numerous benefits of proximity to mission stations and often moved their settlements closer to missions. Carrie Willard, Hudson Stuck, and Russian Orthodox clerics reported Natives requesting missions in their villages. Missionaries appreciated that their access to the children's hearts and minds in the mission schools also translated into tremendous potential for the spread of Christianity as the children matured and became leaders in their villages. Missionaries also clearly understood the effectiveness of Native translators and other "helpers" in spreading the gospel to their own people.

The translation of *Sjutton År i Alaska*, Albin Johnson's memoirs of his seventeen years as a Swedish Evangelical Covenant missionary in Yakutat, thus provides English readers another eyewitness perspective of missionary–Tlingit relations at the turn of the century and of relatively traditional Yakutat Tlingit culture as it was confronted with myriad foreign influences. It is the only such account that depicts the Yakutat Tlingit. Renowned anthropologist Frederica de Laguna made use of Johnson's memoir to create her ethnological masterpiece on the Yakutat Tlingit, *Under Mount Saint Elias*, relying on text that was translated for her. However, *Sjutton År i Alaska* has never been accessible to the general public not fluent in Swedish. L. Arden Almquist, who wrote a brief history of the Covenant's work in Alaska, published in 1962, noted that Johnson's memoir was a rich historical resource that regrettably few could access because it was not available in translation.

ALBIN JOHNSON'S ALASKA

Johnson's audience was the Covenant leadership and mission friends, whom he hoped would be moved to contribute support for the Alaska mission field by learning of the needs of the Tlingit people, the fruit that the missionaries' labor had reaped thus far, and the potential for greater harvests with increased assistance. He clearly hoped that his readership would be inspired by Alaska itself, whose stunning beauty, he wrote, was yet largely undiscovered. Indeed, one of the most striking features of the memoir is the awe that southeast Alaska's dramatic natural beauty inspired in Johnson. *Seventeen Years in Alaska* is replete with passages expressing his wonder at the spectacular scenery. The mountains in particular gave him cause to reflect on the Lord's mastery in creating such grandeur. In fact, he wrote that he was reminded more than once of Carl Boberg's hymn *How Great Thou Art* as he gazed upon the majestic mountains. Likely few Americans realize that this well-known hymn originated in Sweden.

No one could have failed to be moved by Yakutat's setting, but Johnson would have been especially sensitive to his natural surroundings, given his Swedish upbringing. Johnson's memoir presents an impression of an idyllic childhood in rural southwest Sweden, where he was raised in a loving home, the youngest of seven surviving children in his family. "The free country life" instilled in him a lifelong reverence for nature. His account of the childhood hours, indeed years, he spent running and playing in the out-of-doors, swimming, picking flowers, and later herding the family's sheep exemplifies the Swedish love of nature and outdoor activities.

As is the case today, Swedish culture in the late 1800s esteemed nature: its inherent value as well as the restorative qualities it offered human beings.

In the early twenty-first century, parents still often walk their babies in strollers and place them outside in their carriages to nap because they believe the fresh air promotes good health. They regularly encourage their children to play outside. Classes of schoolchildren take field trips to wander in the forest and learn about the birds and vegetation. *Allemans rätt* grants Swedes the right to traverse private property for recreational purposes and to pick berries and mushrooms in forested areas, and Swedes regularly take advantage of this right. Thus Johnson's Swedish upbringing predisposed him to appreciate southeast Alaska's habitat. However, nothing in his Swedish background could have prepared him for the breathtaking mountains, fjords, glaciers, and waterfalls of the Yakutat region or for the abundant wildlife he found there. Southern Sweden by comparison was pastoral, with rolling hills, lakes, and forests, and it was settled with small farm communities. Alaska's spectacular sunsets and mesmerizing northern lights also surpassed those in the Nordic countries in Johnson's estimation. His emphasis on Alaska's natural environment undoubtedly reflected Johnson's sincere appreciation of its unparalleled beauty. Consciously or unconsciously, Johnson likely also sensed the landscape's ability to inspire his readers to come to the aid of the mission and Alaska's indigenous peoples.

Albin Johnson's depiction of his seventeen years in Alaska as a Swedish Covenant missionary during the late nineteenth and early twentieth centuries illustrates the religious, educational, medical, and social welfare functions that Covenant and other missionaries performed, along with providing a rendering of social and environmental conditions in southeast Alaska at the time. While at times Johnson's words ring with paternalism and ethnocentrism now, attitudes at which the twenty-first-century reader chafes, his account leaves no doubt of his and the Covenant's commitment to the well-being of Alaska Natives. Missionaries' devotion to and investment in the indigenous peoples of Alaska stood in stark contrast to the United States government's anemic efforts to meet its obligations to Alaska Natives under its "trust relationship," especially given the overwhelming social, economic, and human health consequences of the waves of migration of Americans and others to Alaska following its purchase in 1867.

Svenska Missionsförbundet, or the Swedish Mission Covenant, was founded in 1878 in the context of the evangelical free-church movement of nineteenth-century Sweden. The free-church movement arose in response to the Swedish Lutheran Church's rigidity, corruption, oppressiveness, and "dead formalism" that did not attend to congregants' spiritual needs,[10] as well as in response to international influences. The free-church principle emphasized the Bible itself as the one true source of Christian belief and that individuals could interpret the Bible themselves. Those actively engaged in the movement were known by a number of terms, including Believers, Readers, Friends, and Mission Friends, because they tended to express much enthusiasm for evangelism, including foreign missions.[11] The Swedish Mission Covenant was a federation of local "communities of believers" who adhered to free-church principles as well as to the conviction that the true Christian church consisted only of those who had experienced personal conversion.[12]

According to Covenant historian Karl Olsson, the Swedish Covenant became interested in Alaska in response to recent attention given to northern indigenous peoples and their needs in the face of Euro-American migration to the region. Noting Alaska Eskimos' needs, the great Finnish-Swedish explorer A. E. Nordensjiöld reportedly contacted E. J. Ekman, one of the founding pastors of the church in Sweden, who in 1877 had proclaimed the need for missionary work "among the heathen" and who had specifically expressed an interest in the Arctic. Pioneer missionary Sheldon Jackson's *Alaska*, published in 1880, also had made a strong impression on people interested in mission work.[13]

Alaska became the Covenant of Sweden's first mission field when in 1887, the Swedish Axel Karlson began missionary work in Unalakleet on the Seward Peninsula after having been invited there by Eskimos he met in St. Michael.[14] The following year missionaries Adolph Lydell and Karl Johan Henrikson, also from Sweden, established a mission in Yakutat.[15] In May 1889, Albin Johnson arrived in Yakutat to replace the ailing Lydell.

Having been born in southwest Sweden in 1865, Johnson had been profoundly impacted by the religious revival that swept through Sweden in the mid-nineteenth century. His father had experienced a dramatic conversion and had become a follower of the pietistic Henric Schartau. The family sometimes traveled to nearby Jönköping, a center of revivalist activity at the time, to listen to evangelists or colporteurs.[16] At a young age Johnson came to believe that God could make a preacher or missionary of him.

Following his confirmation in the state Lutheran Church in Velinge, at about the age of 14, Johnson moved to Jönköping, found work, and attended Christian gatherings in the community. He seems to have had a dramatic conversion experience, after which he traveled to Norrland, where he became a colporteur.[17] Later Johnson applied to the Swedish Mission Covenant's mission school in Kristinehamn and was accepted. Upon his graduation three years later he was ordained and sent on a mission to Alaska. In the meantime he had become engaged to marry Agnes Wallin of Jönköping.[18]

Johnson expressed no regret at leaving Sweden but rather delight in responding to the call. Directly after being assigned his mission, he embarked on his journey to America. After studying English in San Francisco for just two weeks, he proceeded to Alaska.

Upon his arrival in Yakutat, Johnson was taken aback by the appearance of the Natives who besieged the ship's passengers with demands for alcohol and tobacco. Yet his memoir reveals that his heart quickly warmed to the people, and he developed genuine affection for his Tlingit flock. This devotion can be seen not only in his portrayal of their strengths and endearing qualities but in his advocacy for their interests.

The very remote Yakutat lay on the northeastern shore of the Gulf of Alaska on the eastern side of Yakutat Bay in an area rich in aquatic and land-based fauna, with lush vegetation including wild strawberries, blueberries, salmonberries, and cranberries that were nourished by heavy precipitation. Bears were especially numerous in the area, as were mountain goats and a wide variety of sea life, including sea otter, fur seals, and salmon. The nearby Mount Saint Elias dominated the landscape.

The Tlingit of southeast Alaska, whose territory extends along most of Alaska's Panhandle, are divided into two exogamous moieties, the Raven and Wolf-Eagle, and four major groups: the Southern, Northern, Inland (who migrated centuries ago into what is now the Yukon Territory), and Gulf Coast, the last group being the Yakutat Tlingit. Each group is organized matrilineally.[19] The Yakutat have identified as Tlingit for centuries, but their dialect and area place names reveal that they descend from Eyak and Ahtna Athabaskans of the middle Copper River who moved southeast into the Yakutat area centuries ago and were dominated by Tlingit.[20]

Amid the abundance of natural resources in the region, the Yakutat Tlingit had long been self-reliant. Their relatively sedentary lifestyle afforded them time to craft marketable items, and they were avid and shrewd traders with travelers on the ships that visited Yakutat. Among the arts and crafts the Tlingit made were carved wooden bowls inlaid with mother-of-pearl shells; knives with elaborately carved bone handles, some with copper blades; moccasins; and baskets. Yakutat basketry was recognized as the finest of all Tlingit craft work.[21] The Tlingit were master canoe builders as well. Owing to the wealth of renewable resources in the region and to the Tlingit's craftsmanship and skill in trading, they lived in relative comfort. Despite these advantages, the Tlingit suffered from the high disease and mortality rates that plagued Alaska Natives following contact with Euro-Americans, owing to their low immunity and to poor sanitary conditions and ventilation in homes.

In 1889 when Johnson arrived, Yakutat consisted of two communities; the store run by a Sitka merchant and the mission site were on the mainland and had attracted some Tlingit settlers there. One chief lived on the mainland and the other lived across Monti Bay at Port Mulgrave on the southeastern end of Khantaak Island. The latter, older village consisted of six houses.[22] When the mission station was completed later that year, many of the Tlingit moved from the older village on Khantaak Island to be close to the mission house and store.[23]

Meanwhile, just before Johnson had entered the Swedish Covenant's mission school in Kristinehamn, the Swedish Evangelical Mission Covenant in America had been established in Chicago in 1885. The flood of Swedish immigrants arriving in America in the 1860s and 1870s had been influenced by the spiritual revivals taking place in their homeland. Many sought Swedish congregations in America;[24] those in the Midwest who had misgivings about the Church of Sweden formed independent congregations in Chicago and nearby areas. Their pastors tended to be self-educated, and congregations stressed leading a Christ-like life over questions of doctrine. In 1885 at a meeting of representatives of various Lutheran-associated congregations and other independent Mission Friends congregations, attendees formed the Swedish Evangelical Mission Covenant in America.[25] The four central principles of the American Mission Covenant were (1) that church activities be directed toward spiritual life, (2) commitment to evangelism at home and among the pagan peoples of the world, (3) membership in local churches dependent only upon true belief, not adherence to any specific doctrines or creeds, and (4) the Bible's being the only infallible authoritative source for believers.[26]

In 1889 Covenant missionaries in Alaska requested that responsibility for the Alaska missions be transferred from the Covenant in Sweden to the American Covenant. They received most of their funding from the American organization, and communication was easier with the American Covenant. The Swedish Mission Covenant agreed and the transfer took place that year.[27]

According to Covenant historian Karl Olsson, owing largely to Karlson's and Lydell's reports of the rapid spread of Christianity among the Tlingit and Eskimos, "the Alaska mission was everybody's darling," and the Swedish Covenant in America sent several more missionaries to Alaska and established additional missions on the Seward Peninsula and schools at Unalakleet and Yakutat.[28] Agnes Wallin joined Johnson in 1891, having traveled seven thousand miles from Jönköping to marry him and join him in his work. They were wed just after she arrived. The captain of the ship as well as some of the passengers went ashore to witness the ceremony. She later related how strange and lonely she felt as she watched the ship pull away.[29] Her anxiety must have been overwhelming. She spoke no English,[30] she had entered a completely foreign environment and social context, she had wed a man she had not seen in at least two years, and she was beginning a new life as the wife of a missionary and pastor. Agnes Wallin Johnson was not yet twenty-seven years old on this day in May 1891. Her initial anxiety notwithstanding, she devoted herself to her new role and to the community, and she came to love the people of Yakutat.[31]

THE YAKUTAT MISSION

Mission work had begun in Yakutat almost immediately following Lydell's and Henrikson's arrival with supplies in 1888. Lydell reportedly purchased the log trading post from a trader, Doctor Ballou. Until the church and mission buildings were constructed, they held gatherings in the large Native houses on Khantaak Island. The communication barrier was one of the greatest initial challenges to the missionaries' objectives. English was their lingua franca, but neither the missionaries nor the Tlingit were fully conversant in English, especially in the first years of the Covenant's work in Yakutat. To Albin Johnson, who had had but two weeks of training in English in San Francisco before his arrival in Yakutat, the language of the Tlingit sounded especially alien. "Such strange throat sounds!" he wrote of his first impression. Almost none of the Tlingit spoke English, so the missionaries engaged children and young people to serve as translators.[32] Their first interpreter was a youth from Sitka named Jeme Ka-kaashra. His eagerness to hear the missionaries' message and his faithfulness compensated for his less than perfect English, which of course improved over time. The Word spread remarkably quickly, and one after another Tlingit, and eventually groups of them, stood up during services and renounced their former "heathen" ways. The missionaries naturally were delighted to welcome their new congregants into the fold.[33]

Seven years after Agnes Wallin Johnson's arrival, the language challenges between the missionaries and Tlingit were still notable enough that Arthur Dietz wrote in his gold rush memoir of his visit in Yakutat, "The missionaries were also attempting to teach the natives English, but were not succeeding very well, because both Mr. Johnson and his wife spoke with a decided Swedish accent and the natives, of course, talked in much the same way."[34] Alaska historian Terrence Cole has labeled Dietz's account of his experience in the Klondike "the greatest fake gold rush memoir ever written"; in fact, it is not even clear that Arthur Dietz wrote the book.[35] However, Dietz and his group of gold seekers did sail from Seattle to Yakutat in February 1898, from where they planned to climb the Malaspina Glacier to reach the Klondike (a creative idea, indeed!), and the general account of their landing in Yakutat and the Johnsons' hospitality rings true.

The Johnsons continued to use Tlingit translators throughout their years in Yakutat. In 1904 and 1905 Johnson praised the skill and dedication of their loyal translator Paul Italio: "He is a very faithful and zealous young man with uncommonly clean, strong, and Christian character. He preaches himself and prays for his people with burning zeal. We are happy to have him in our service." Johnson acknowledged the great value of indigenous employees, alluding to the heightened credibility of Native proselytizers among their own people.[36] He noted approvingly that Italio had expressed a wish to be a missionary and dedicate himself completely to the mission.[37] In the same vein, the phenomenon of the Native "criers" who fell into trances marked a turning point in the mission's work as Natives themselves spread the Word. Johnson by this time had learned some Tlingit, as evidenced by his use of a number of Tlingit phrases in his memoir. When a translator was not available, as occurred for an extended period in the fall of 1899, Johnson provided services in Tlingit as best as he could.[38]

By the summer of 1889 Yakutat's mission house was completed, and an orphanage housed five boys.[39] In 1891 the missionaries built a two-story building that housed twenty-four orphans and included living quarters for the missionaries, as well as a schoolroom that doubled as a sanctuary.[40] In January 1893 disaster struck: the building burned to the ground with virtually all of the mission's and the missionaries' valuables. Henrikson reported that the greatest tragedy was their no longer being able to house the children in their home. The mission was able to keep only five girls.[41]

Fortunately, the previous fall Henrikson had acquired a steam saw that had not been assembled yet. The missionaries quickly built a house for the mill, chopping the logs and sawing the boards by hand, with the assistance of Natives. Johnson related in his memoir that once the saw was operating, the Tlingit stood in awe of its capabilities. They were inspired to build new houses for themselves, and the missionaries sawed the boards and taught the Natives to build. Within a couple of years Yakutat was transformed from a village of simple haphazardly placed dwellings to one with well-built frame houses in orderly rows.[42] Henrikson's engineering and carpentry skills were legendary. More than a half century later, the Tlingit of Yakutat remembered him, especially for his energy and building skills.[43] After leaving Yakutat in 1899 to serve in the northern Covenant mission field on the Seward Peninsula, Henrikson put his talents to work in building at Unalakleet, Golovin, and Elim as well as preaching and teaching. He served over thirty years in Alaska.[44]

The Tlingit readily took to carpentry and built furniture for their new homes, as well. Covenant Secretary David Nyvall wrote approvingly in an 1897 report, "In one word, the mill has proven an effective help in civilizing the natives and thereby opening a way for the Christian mission among them," illustrating the explicit common purposes of the U.S. government and the missions in civilizing Alaska Natives.[45] Nyvall's report also evidenced the ways in which the material advantages the missionaries could offer enhanced their relationships with the Natives and perhaps the appeal of their Christian message. By 1897, thirty-eight Natives had been baptized in Yakutat. Between sixty and a hundred children attended the mission school, which opened additional avenues of influence among the Tlingit.[46]

As was the case throughout Alaska, the evangelistic, educational, and medical roles of the missionaries intertwined. As teachers the missionaries were authority figures, and their lessons encompassed the three R's, along with hygiene and morality, including temperance ideology, all of which promoted health and reinforced the usefulness of the Christian message. The Bureau of Education considered its appointees, most of whom either were missionaries or were recommended by the churches in the respective villages, as much social workers as teachers. They were expected to work with adults and families in their homes in addition to teaching the children at school.[47] The missionaries' ability to heal built trust, which also enhanced the plausibility of their spiritual teachings. Vaccines and surgeries, the benefits of which shamans could not effect, especially impressed Alaska Natives.

Covenant mission accounts suggest that the Tlingit were eager to learn from the missionaries but perplexed by their notions of sin. Especially confounding was the prohibition against alcohol, given that white men had introduced the substance. The missionaries insisted that the Bible forbade both drinking and dancing, but convincing the Tlingit of the evils of alcohol was no easy task.[48] U.S. Army Lt. W. R. Abercrombie, who had led a reconnaissance expedition in the region, wrote in 1884 that the Yakutat Tlingit were "exceedingly fond" of *hoochenoo,* the homemade liquor that U.S. soldiers had taught Alaska Natives to make.[49] The temptation to indulge in alcohol and participate in other forbidden activities, even for those who had converted, was great, and many "reformed" Natives "backslid" again. "The poor people, they are torn between two masters," wrote Johnson.[50] During Johnson's tenure in Yakutat a youth organization formed to support members in their efforts to resist returning to former practices, such as drinking alcohol and participating in "heathen" dancing.[51] Backsliders often rejoined the fold, as Johnson reported with evident satisfaction in 1900: "Many of those that had gone astray during their feasts before Christmas have returned."[52]

Johnson tried, throughout his years in Yakutat, to stop the liquor traffic, frequently reporting alcohol violations to the government, which was not without risk to himself.[53] However, positive results appear to have been temporary. On numerous occasions he confronted distillers and bootleggers and often these men threatened him with violence.[54] Agnes Johnson and missionary Jenny Olson also showed remarkable courage in carrying out a "Carrie Nation" campaign against a bootlegger in the community.

Cannery, saw mill, and railroad work, along with sales of handcrafted items, allowed Yakutat residents to earn cash, much of which went to whiskey peddlers.[55] Law enforcement was too sporadic to deter bootlegging, although the Indian police system provided some law and order in southeast Alaska.[56] Economic development expanded, especially after the turn of the century, with salteries and new canneries opening. By 1901 Yakutat was completely inundated with outsiders who disturbed any semblance of tranquility in the village. "Boats come and go, loaded with people of every sort. The most dangerous for us are those who come to attach themselves to the Natives in one way or another, ruin and humiliate their women, sell them liquor, convince them of such things as there is no God and that we only teach them untruths, and so on. These are in general morally bankrupt people," Johnson wrote.[57] In 1901 Johnson sent a plea to authorities to intervene, and in response Captain William Kilgore of the *Rush* brought Governor Brady and Commissioner Edward DeGroff from Sitka to Yakutat to investigate. Six people were sentenced to jail time in Sitka, including the captain of the *Newport,* which had been anchored at Yakutat selling liquor. Before Commissioner DeGroff had come ashore, a white man who had been living illegally with a Native woman for several years went to Johnson's house and asked him to marry them. Before the *Rush* left Yakutat, Johnson had married, in one ceremony, the rest of the mixed-race couples who were living together in violation of the law. He anticipated that the white men would no longer be able to abandon their Native partners as easily as they often did. At the request of the commissioner, Johnson traveled to Sitka to testify regarding some of the worst crimes.[58] This was apparently the first time that the law had been applied in Yakutat, and Governor Brady speculated that both whites and Natives had come to believe that it never would be enforced.[59]

Economic development expanded markedly with the dawning of the twentieth century. Residents at Yakutat found employment opportunities at two salteries, at the cannery, and with the Yakutat and Southern Railroad Company. Johnson wrote in 1904 that most of the local Natives worked for Yakutat and Southern: "Our Natives are well appreciated in their work and earn $2.25 a day in wages." Johnson clearly was ambivalent about the economic development. In many ways it made the missionaries' work more difficult. In addition to the corrupting influences of Western civilization, "there is so much planning and speculating in Alaska that the people don't have time to think about God or saving their souls," he wrote in his 1904 annual report.[60]

In addition to the continuous struggle against alcohol, which was the missionaries' greatest challenge, fornication, adultery, and dancing were the main "social problems" that Covenant missionaries battled, both in winning souls and in retaining them.[61] By the turn of the twentieth century the American Covenant leadership had come to view Americans as hedonistic, and they grew increasingly adamant about resisting degeneracy, such as card playing, dancing, the theater, and moving pictures.[62] Christian missionaries constantly sought to protect Alaska Natives from negative influences of whites. Johnson wrote of the "loathsome and corrupting" illnesses that the white men brought with them to Alaska. Ernest Larson, Covenant missionary at Unalakleet, lamented in 1935, "Whence come drinking, tobacco, swearing, gambling, bad movies, modern dancing and all that goes with it? Ungodly whites brought and are bringing these evils to Alaska."[63]

Missionaries tried to protect Native girls and young women from the many single (or unaccompanied) men who entered the territory. Native girls who had been brought up in the mission schools and had consequently adopted some Western habits were especially attractive to white men. Olsson wrote that girls schooled by the missions "were not only seduced by white adventurers... but were also courted as prospective wives by both whites and natives."[64] Governor Brady, who had come to Alaska as a missionary, noted that the missionaries had found this to be "the worst drawback to their work." It was difficult to "preserve" the mission-educated young Native women "as wives for the young (Native) men."[65]

Covenant missionaries also did their best to abolish the traditional Native practice of polygamy. The executive board of the Mission Covenant in America declared emphatically that polygamy must not be permitted among Christians, and it encouraged missionaries to assist in the amicable resolution of the matter between men and multiple wives, while recognizing the first wife as the legal spouse. Many Native men considered themselves fortunate to have more than one wife; however, American law backed the missionaries.[66]

Teaching Native children proved to be challenging, owing partly to what Alaska Governor Lyman Knapp termed the children's and parents' "natural indifference," especially during the fall and spring months when subsistence activities drew families away from villages.[67] Education authorities agreed to a shortened school year. To improve attendance during the adjusted school year, General Education Agent Sheldon Jackson, several governors, and Alaska's schoolteachers and superintendents reportedly unanimously supported a compulsory education law.[68] Beginning in 1891, along with working to preserve the peace, Indian police encouraged children's attendance at school, reportedly with some positive effect.[69]

Governor Knapp praised missionaries' work in Alaska, particularly their educational efforts. Though he endorsed the general principle of separation of church and state, given the national government's unwillingness to expend additional funds to educate Alaska Native children, he declared that "these noble agencies" (the missions) should be encouraged in their educational efforts.[70] Knapp wrote that he knew of no school that was more deserving of funding or had shown better results than the Swedish boarding and day school at Yakutat.[71] Governor Knapp's successor, James Sheakley, was equally complimentary of missionaries' work in education: "Nothing has contributed to ameliorate the hard condition of the Indian in Alaska so much as the work of the missionary and the introduction of Government schools."[72]

The Covenant missions in Yakutat and on the Seward Peninsula enjoyed strong relationships with Alaska's governors and with General Education Agent Sheldon Jackson, a man of strong personality and convictions who was and continues to be praised in some quarters and condemned in others. His biographer, J. Arthur Lazell, dubbed him the "Alaskan Apostle," and the former Presbyterian missionary Governor John Brady especially appreciated him, but many people resented the broad scope of his authority and particularly his work to enforce liquor regulations. Believing that appointing Christian law enforcers was the best way—perhaps the only way—to bring law and order to Alaska, Jackson continuously lobbied authorities in Washington, D.C., to appoint Christian federal officers, and he never backed down from his stance on the prohibition of liquor.[73] Both of these positions accorded well with the view of Covenant mission personnel, and they appreciated as well Jackson's efforts to extend educational opportunities to Alaska Native children in co-operation with Christian missions. Moreover, Covenant mission stations on the Seward Peninsula were directly engaged in the reindeer herding project Jackson initiated.[74]

The Covenant missionaries' healing obligation was perhaps the most daunting of their objectives in Alaska. As diseases ravaged Native villages, the Native population received little medical care aside from that donated by military doctors or administered by missionaries. Alaska governors repeatedly urged Congress to provide medical care for the Native population, but to little avail.[75] Between 1891 and 1900, physicians eventually were posted at twenty-five Alaska communities; more than half of these were missionary doctors. Churches and missionaries were often the first to build and maintain hospitals in Native and mining communities; for instance, the Covenant built a hospital in Unalakleet.[76] Covenant missionary Dr. C. O. Lind served at Golovin from 1901 to 1902 and then moved to Unalakleet, where he worked as doctor, reindeer herder, teacher, and Sunday school superintendent. The Mission Covenant stationed nurses at its mission stations as well.[77] Other missionaries oftentimes had little or no medical training, however. Moreover, the medicine that physicians had at their disposal was of little more use than the treatments that shamans might have used; their basic drugs of any significant value were morphine, digitalis, and mercury, along with the smallpox vaccine. Antiseptic practices during medical procedures also saved lives.[78]

Alaska Natives suffered from high rates of tuberculosis, eye disease, and venereal diseases and from periodic devastating influenza epidemics. In 1900 the measles accompanied the flu, rendering it all the more deadly.[79] Tuberculosis spread terror in Yakutat, owing to unsanitary conditions and because many families lived together in large, one-room houses. The Johnsons did their best to attend to the medical needs of Yakutat residents. They made house calls to care for the ill and brought them meals. Like other missionaries and teachers, the Johnsons taught the Natives hygiene and sanitation to guard against the spread of disease. In addition to their explicit lessons on sanitation, the Johnsons constantly sought to set a good example for the Tlingit by keeping the mission buildings and grounds neat and tidy.[80]

Agnes Johnson was intimately involved in all of these mission functions. She nurtured many children at the orphanage and school, and she participated actively in the church and community. She taught girls to sew, and she sewed clothing for them. She sewed dresses for Chief George's wife and taught her how to make bread. Mrs. Johnson often made home visits simply to check on people and encourage them to come to church. The Johnsons invited members of the community to their home for meals as well, demonstrating their hospitality and the warmth they felt for the Tlingit people.

Mrs. Johnson learned to play the organ while living in Yakutat so that she could play during the services and accompany the choir. Johnson wrote frequently in his annual reports of how musical the Tlingit were, how they loved to sing, and how much the music brightened the mission's worship services: "they all seem to have singing voices."[81] If what Arthur Dietz wrote about Johnson's poor singing abilities was true, Johnson may have thought it especially remarkable that the Tlingit had such naturally pleasant singing voices.[82] The music actually drew the people to the church services, he wrote.

In addition to nurturing members of the community and the children in the Covenant mission home, Agnes mothered the Johnsons' own two children. Donald Alfons Dettion Johnson was born in Sitka in 1894, and Ruth Hazel Jagestat Johnson was born in 1897 while the Johnsons were on leave in Chicago.[83] The mission took in and cared for orphaned children and others whose parents could not care for them until 1904, when economic conditions improved so much that families could take care of their own children.[84] Johnson wrote in his yearly reports of the energy his wife directed to the mission station and their flock, mentioning from time to time that her duties left her feeling rather frail and drained. The Covenant granted the Johnsons' request to spend the summer of 1902 in Chicago to rest and restore their energies.[85]

AFTER YAKUTAT

The Johnsons left their post as missionaries in Yakutat in June 1905 and settled in North Park, Illinois, where they joined the North Park Covenant congregation. Their children's education reportedly was a primary motivation for returning to the Chicago area, although their health had suffered, as well.[86] A third child was born to the Johnsons in 1907 in Chicago: Sheldon Roland Albin Johnson, named for Presbyterian missionary and education chief in Alaska Sheldon Jackson.[87]

The Johnson family after they moved to North Park, Illinois, with children Donald and Ruth, who were born while the Johnsons lived in Yakutat, and Sheldon, who was born in 1907 in Chicago. Courtesy of Covenant Archives and Historical Library, North Park University, Chicago, Illinois.

Albin Johnson maintained a full work schedule for the following twenty years. He traveled to raise funds for the Covenant's foreign missions the first year and then returned to Yakutat for the year 1906–1907, after which he again traveled in the interest of the foreign missions. For thirteen years, from 1908 to 1921, Johnson served as the superintendent of the Covenant hospital and retirement home in North Park. Subsequently he filled posts as temporary pastor at Covenant churches in Warren, Minnesota, followed by Hartford, New Haven, and New Britain, Connecticut, whereupon he retired in 1925 at the age of sixty, having been in Covenant service for thirty-four years.[88] He had published his memoir in 1924. Thereafter until his death, he was known among Swedish Covenanters as "Sjutton År i Alaska Johnson," likely partly in friendly jest; after all, publishing one's memoirs requires a certain level of hubris. The moniker also aided those in the Swedish community in Chicago in differentiating Albin Johnson from the many Johnsons in their midst.

The Johnsons remained in Chicago for the rest of their lives. Their retirement was marred by the death of their daughter Ruth in 1927 at the age of thirty. Mrs. Johnson's health began to fail in 1942. After several weeks in the Swedish Covenant Hospital, Donald took his mother into his home and cared for her until her death in 1945.[89] Albin Johnson survived his wife by two years; he died in September 1947 at the age of eighty-two.[90]

Albin Johnson's seventeen years at Yakutat left a lasting impression on him. His memoir, written nearly two decades after his departure, evokes

Albin and Agnes Johnson in their golden years in North Park, Illinois. Courtesy of Covenant Archives and Historical Library, North Park University, Chicago, Illinois.

images of a young man who arrived in the village woefully uneducated in Tlingit culture. Yet his deep spiritual convictions inspired and compelled him to share the gospel with "pagan" people whose fate seemed all but sealed with the influx of non-Native migrants to the region. His yearly reports and his memoir reveal a man who saw himself as a servant of God, who eagerly accepted the onerous responsibilities of his work, and who rejoiced in the fruits of his labor, all the while giving full credit to God. He left the comfortable world he knew for a completely foreign one where he perceived the people to have great unmet needs. His affection for and devotion to the people seemed to grow with the challenges and with his increased sense of the urgency of protecting them from disease and corruption. The flow of liquor and gold seekers into the village rose sharply following the discovery of gold in the Klondike in 1897. At the dawn of the twentieth century, economic development expanded in Yakutat, boat traffic increased, and, as Johnson wrote, civilization advanced faster than the Natives could comprehend its implications. There were always plenty of whites eager to sell Natives liquor and seduce the women. Given the constant pressure to be led astray, it was essential to "pray and work among (the Natives) so that they might completely come over to the Lord's side," Johnson wrote in 1904.[91]

As for the Johnsons' impact on the community of Yakutat and the Tlingit's perception of the mission, surely opinions varied. However, it seems that most community members understood that the missionaries sought to help and serve the community. Soon after the mission was planted, residents moved from the old village on Khantaak Island to be closer to the mission. The Yakutat Tlingit undoubtedly appreciated the kindness and generosity of the Johnsons and other missionaries and found their promises of eternal life attractive and the social and economic benefits of close ties with the mission appealing. Johnson sensed that Yakutat residents especially appreciated the home visits he and his wife made to the ill and simply to check on people. "They are always happy when we come and laugh so heartily," he reported.[92] Just how complete their conversion was is uncertain, of course. Johnson himself was reluctant to report the size of his congregation, noting how impressionable the Tlingit were, how they could exclaim their faith and pray for forgiveness for their sins one week and "backslide" the next. Frederica de Laguna wrote of the enduring traditional spirituality within the Covenant flock in Yakutat: "In the hearts of those who went regularly to church the earnest preachings of Johnson and Henrikson had not been able to erase the deep-grained fearful confidence in the shaman, or terror of the witch and Land Otter Man."[93] Likely syncretism had taken place, as anthropologist Ernest Burch found had occurred among the Iñupiat as they adopted Christianity at the turn of the twentieth century.[94]

EPILOGUE: THE SWEDISH MISSION COVENANT AND THIS VOLUME

The Swedish Evangelical Mission Covenant impacted much more broadly its northern Alaska field on and near the Seward Peninsula, where the Covenant established several mission stations, an orphanage, and a hospital. It also became actively involved in the reindeer husbandry program that Sheldon Jackson had initiated to supplement the Natives' food sources as well as encourage their "civilization." In the twenty-first century, reindeer herding is still practiced on the Seward Peninsula and several Covenant churches are active in the region.

The gold rush that began at the turn of the twentieth century on the Seward Peninsula brought tens of thousands of non-Native migrants to the region and lured Covenant missionaries from their posts to search for the coveted mineral. The frenzy for gold embroiled the Mission Covenant of America in litigation that distracted the leadership and tarnished its reputation for decades, hindering the Covenant's ability to raise funds for its missions.[95] Despite this cloud that loomed over the church, the Covenant in Alaska continued to grow, especially on the Seward Peninsula, and Natives increasingly took leadership roles in the churches.

In 1954, the Swedish Mission Covenant agreed to trade its mission at Yakutat for the Presbyterian post at Wales on the Seward Peninsula, allowing each denomination to consolidate its posts. In 1960, thirteen Alaska churches operated under the umbrella of the Swedish Mission Covenant. They were located in Nome, White Mountain, Golovin, Wales, Elim, Koyuk, Shaktoolik, Unalakleet, Marshall, Hooper Bay, Scammon Bay, Mountain Village, and Mekoryuk, none of which are on Alaska's road system.[96] In 2013, the Evangelical Covenant Church of Alaska (ECCA) lists on its website eight churches on Alaska's road system, seven churches in the Norton Sound region, and five churches in the Yukon Delta. ECCA also operates the Alaska Christian College in Soldotna, the Covenant Bible Camp at Unalakleet, and radio station KICY in Nome.[97] This expansion illustrates the church's enduring influence in rural Alaska and its extension into more urban areas as Alaska's population has become increasingly urban.

Following the Johnsons' departure in 1905, Covenant missionaries Edward Anton Rasmuson and Jenny Olson continued the preaching, teaching, and healing work the Johnsons had done for seventeen years at Yakutat. Olson had arrived in 1901 from Sköttkärn in Värmland, Sweden, and Rasmuson had arrived from Minneapolis after immigrating from Blekinge, Sweden, in 1901. He had attended the Skogsbergh School established by Swedish Covenant pastor Erik August Skogsbergh, after which he was recommended by the

Covenant to be a teacher in Yakutat. Along with teaching, Rasmuson shared preaching and missionary work with Albin Johnson the first winter. The following spring Johnson married Rasmuson and Olson before the Johnsons left to settle in Chicago.[98]

Rasmuson served as teacher and missionary until 1909 when he was relieved of his teaching duties, because the government wanted to distinguish the roles of pastors and teachers more clearly.[99] Edward and Jenny Rasmuson continued to serve as missionaries until they left Yakutat in 1914 to move

Portrait of Jenny Olson Rasmuson within *A Cry in the Wilderness* by Rie Muñoz, commissioned by Elmer Rasmuson. The mural, which hangs in the Elmer E. Rasmuson Library at the University of Alaska Fairbanks, depicts numerous missionaries among the Alaska Native peoples they served in the late 1800s and early 1900s.

to Minnesota.[100] The Rasmusons' family had grown during their tenure in Yakutat with the births of Maud Evangeline in 1906 in Sitka and Elmer in 1909 in Yakutat.[101] The Rasmusons served the people of Yakutat in the same selfless manner that the Johnsons had, battling liquor peddlers and disease and welcoming the people into their hearts. While living in Yakutat Edward Rasmuson, in particular, developed numerous civic and other capacities that would serve him well throughout his later life.

After leaving Yakutat in 1914, E.A. Rasmuson was admitted to the Bar Association in Minnesota. In 1915 he and Jenny returned to Alaska, where he planned to practice law. The following year Rasmuson passed the Alaska bar exam and was appointed commissioner in Skagway.[102] Two years later, he was asked to take over the leadership of the failing National Bank of Alaska. He served as president and director of the bank from 1918 to 1944, after which he was chairman of the board. During his years at the helm, Rasmuson built the National Bank of Alaska into the largest bank in the state. Rasmuson held numerous other leadership positions in the territory, along with serving as the Swedish vice consul for Alaska for many years. He was knighted by the king of Sweden in 1937.[103] Ten years later, reflecting on their experience in Yakutat, Rasmuson wrote, "We both consider these years the happiest, most satisfactory and best remunerative years of our lives; would not have missed them for anything."[104]

Edward and Jenny Rasmuson's son Elmer assumed leadership of the National Bank of Alaska as president in 1943; in 1965 he was elected chairman of the board of directors, a role he filled until he retired in 1974. His son Edward became chairman of the board in 1985.[105] The Rasmuson family followed the course set by their Swedish immigrant and Alaska pioneer forebears in public service. Together with his mother, Elmer Rasmuson established the Rasmuson Foundation in 1955 to improve the quality of life of Alaskans. In the early twenty-first century it is the largest foundation in Alaska and awards $20 million annually to a variety of nonprofit entities to further its mission. At his death in 2000 at the age of ninety-one, Elmer Rasmuson left his $400 million personal fortune to the Rasmuson Foundation.[106] During his lifetime Rasmuson also endowed the library at the University of Alaska's flagship campus in Fairbanks that bears his name.[107] The foundation also provided a $500,000 grant to fund translations of historical Alaska literature. This translation of Albin Johnson's *Sjutton År i Alaska* is being published by the University of Alaska Press as a part of the Rasmuson Historical Translation Series project and can be seen as an outgrowth of the Mission Covenant's and the Rasmuson family's dedication to service to Alaskans.

NOTES

1. Anatolii Kamenskii, *Tlingit Indians of Alaska*, 121.
2. Andrei A. Znamenski, *Through Orthodox Eyes*, 26.
3. Carrie M. Willard, *Carrie M. Willard Among the Tlingits*, 20. They named the mission site after the secretary of the Presbyterian Woman's Executive Committee of Home Missions. The Willards had chosen a neutral location on Portage Bay, rather than any of the four Chilkat villages in the area, to avoid presumptions of favoritism and consequent jealousy.
4. John Wight Chapman, *A Camp on the Yukon*, 194–194.
5. Hudson Stuck, *Ten Thousand Miles With a Dog Sled*, 189, 352.
6. Ann Fienup-Riordan, *The Yup'ik Eskimos*, x.
7. Brevig Mission was named after the missionary's wife, Julia, who dedicated many years to the mission's work and the Iñupiat people and who died at the site in 1908; J. Walter Johnshoy, *Apaurak in Alaska*, 254. The Brevigs also lost two infant children while serving at the mission.
8. Mary Joseph Calasanctius, *The Voice of Alaska*, 323, 324.
9. Ibid., 319.
10. Hjalmar Sundquist, "The Mission Covenanters," 23.
11. Ibid., 34.
12. Charles Milton Strom, *The Swedish Evangelical Mission Covenant Church of America*, 12. The emphasis on personal conversion and true belief contrasted with the state church concept whereby all people born in Sweden automatically were enrolled as members of the Lutheran Church, regardless of their faith.
13. Karl A. Olsson, *By One Spirit*, 411–413.
14. Almquist, *Covenant Missions in Alaska*, 19; Ernest B. Larson, "Our Alaska Mission," 154.
15. Lydell was sent by the Mission Covenant in Sweden. He had traveled with Karlson the previous year and they had stopped in Yakutat, after which Lydell returned to the States to acquire supplies to establish a mission in Yakutat. During this journey Lydell met K. J. Henrikson in Oregon. Henrikson offered to join the mission work in Alaska, and he was thus called by the Mission Covenant in Sweden to serve (Svenska Missionsförbundet i Amerika, *Alaska Förr och Nu*, 75). In various sources Henrikson's name is spelled "Hendrikson," "Hendricksson," and "Hendrickson." I have used the spelling used by Olsson.
16. Colporteurs were wandering evangelists who met with gatherings of worshipers to spread the gospel and read the Bible together.
17. Norrland was the northernmost (of three) *landsdel* or regions, in Sweden.
18. Obituary, Mrs. Albin Johnson, September 7, 1945, in Albin Johnson, Ministerial Records.
19. De Laguna, *Under Mount Saint Elias*, 15.
20. Ibid., 18.
21. Ibid., 184.
22. Ibid., 197.
23. Ibid., 62–63. Some Tlingit remained at the old village on Khantaak Island until 1893.
24. Sundquist, "The Mission Covenanters," 43.
25. Axel Mellander, "Swedish Mission Friends in America," 67–69.

26. C. V. Bowman, "About the Principles of the Mission Friends."
27. Svenska Missionsförbundet i Amerika, *Alaska Förr och Nu*, 75.
28. Olsson, *By One Spirit*, 421–422.
29. Obituary, Mrs. Albin Johnson, in Johnson, Ministerial Records.
30. De Laguna, *Under Mount Saint Elias*, 198. De Laguna's informants who told her that Mrs. Johnson "didn't speak a word of English" clearly referred to her inability to speak English upon her arrival, as she learned English in the fifteen years she lived in Yakutat, though she likely always spoke with a Swedish accent.
31. Obituary, Mrs. Albin Johnson, in Johnson, Ministerial Records.
32. De Laguna, *Under Mount Saint Elias*, 198–199.
33. Svenska Missionsförbundet i Amerika, *Alaska Förr och Nu*, 78. I have used Johnson's spelling here of the young interpreter's name. In Svenska Missionsförbundet i Amerika, *Alaska Förr och Nu*, his name is spelled "Jemmy Coch-ashra."
34. Arthur Arnold Dietz, *Mad Rush for Gold in Frozen North*, 95.
35. Terrence M. Cole, "Klondike Literature," 14.
36. The Eskimo Ojeark or "Rock" was perhaps the most notable example of the effectiveness of Native Christian evangelists. He traveled and spread the Word for many years in northern Alaska and within the continental United States more than once, accompanied by Covenant missionary Axel Karlson.
37. Albin Johnson, "Missionsrapport från Yakutat," 33–34.
38. Johnson, "Missionen i Yakutat, Alaskamissionen," 75. Johnson noted in this annual report that some of the meaning was lost when he spoke to the people in their own language.
39. Almquist, *Covenant Missions in Alaska,* 131; Isabel S. Shepard, *Cruise of the U.S. Steamer "Rush,"* 231.
40. De Laguna, *Under Mount Saint Elias*, 199.
41. Swedish Evangelical Covenant in America, Minutes of the Ninth Annual Meeting, June 7–11, 1893.
42. David Nyvall, "Swedish Evangelical Mission Covenant's Missions in Alaska," 1624–1625.
43. De Laguna, *Under Mount Saint Elias*, 198.
44. Almquist, *Covenant Missions in Alaska*, 25.
45. Nyvall, "Swedish Evangelical Mission Covenant's Missions in Alaska," 1625.
46. Ibid.
47. Harlan Updegraff, Letter to Mrs. W. E. Young, 29 December 1909.
48. Svenska Missionsförbundet i Amerika, *Alaska Förr och Nu*, 78.
49. De Laguna, *Under Mount Saint Elias*, 186. Abercrombie led a reconnaissance expedition along the Copper River. De Laguna wrote that his descriptions of Yakutat were so detailed that they must have been based on personal observation, though not necessarily his own.
50. Johnson, "Missionsrapport från Yakutat," 34.
51. Svenska Missionsförbundet i Amerika, *Alaska Förr och Nu*, 85.
52. Johnson, "Missionen i Yakutat, Alaskamissionen," 6.
53. Olsson, *By One Spirit*, 427; Almquist, *Covenant Missions in Alaska*, 132.
54. Svenska Missionsförbundet i Amerika, *Alaska Förr och Nu*, 100–102.
55. John Brady, Letter to the Secretary of the Interior, 23 December 1905.

56. In 1904 and 1905, an Indian officer served at Yakutat (Alaska Governor, *Report of the Governor of Alaska to the Secretary of the Interior,* 1904; Alaska Governor, *Report of the Governor of Alaska to the Secretary of the Interior,* 1905), but none served there subsequently.
57. Johnson, "Albin Johnsons missionsrapport från Yakutat."
58. Ibid., 31–32.
59. Brady, (Alaska Governor, *Report of the Governor of Alaska to the Secretary of the Interior,* 1901, 35–36).
60. Johnson, "Missionsrapport från Yakutat," 33.
61. Svenska Missionsförbundet i Amerika, *Alaska Förr och Nu*, 98; Larson, "Our Alaska Mission," 164.
62. Strom, *The Swedish Evangelical Mission Covenant Church of America*, 25, 27, 36, 38, and 39.
63. Larson, "Our Alaska Mission," 164.
64. Olsson, *By One Spirit*, 423.
65. Brady, (Alaska Governor, *Report of the Governor of Alaska to the Secretary of the Interior,* 1897, 205). Governor Brady, who first came to Sitka in 1878 as a missionary and later became a businessman and a commissioner before being appointed by President William McKinley to be Alaska's fifth governor (Hinckley, "'We Are More Truly Heathen than the Natives,'" 28), was thoroughly committed to "protecting and civilizing Alaska's Native people (Alaska Governor, *Report of the Governor of Alaska to the Secretary of the Interior,* 1897, 55). As a missionary he had assisted naval authorities in raids on Native distilleries, and he was chagrined by the exploitation of Tlingit women by miners and seamen (ibid., 41). Brady was an early advocate of Native rights, and he helped establish the Sitka Industrial School to educate Native boys and later girls. He cofounded what became Sheldon Jackson College (ibid., 42, 45–47).
66. Swedish Evangelical Covenant in America, Minutes of the Eighth Annual Meeting, September 15–19, 1892, 32; Olsson, *By One Spirit*, 422.
67. Lyman E. Knapp, (Alaska Governor, *Report of the Governor of Alaska to the Secretary of the Interior,* 1889, 232), citing Judge Keatley, chairman of the school board. In the first years when public education was provided, parents reportedly asked to be paid for sending their children to school. Governor Sheakley later speculated that they may have thought that the children were to be of some assistance to the missionaries/teachers and that the parents therefore should have been compensated (Alaska Governor, *Report of the Governor of Alaska to the Secretary of the Interior,* 1895, 16).
68. Sheldon Jackson, Letter to Lyman E. Knapp, 20 September 1899; Brady, Letter to the Secretary of the Interior, 23 December 1905; Walter E. Clark, (Alaska Governor, *Report of the Governor of Alaska to the Secretary of the Interior,* 1911, 27). Nearly all states and territories had adopted compulsory education policies by the early twentieth century.
69. Knapp, (Alaska Governor, *Report of the Governor of Alaska to the Secretary of the Interior,* 1891, 467–468, 472); Sheakley, (Alaska Governor, *Report of the Governor of Alaska to the Secretary of the Interior,* 1893, 5).
70. Knapp, (Alaska Governor, *Report of the Governor of Alaska to the Secretary of the Interior* 1892, 54). The government paid mission stations $90 per year for each child taken into a children's home and $30 per year for each child enrolled in day school. In 1896 the Bureau of Education began paying the Covenant missionaries, as well

as others, $500 per year to teach in schools serving Native children. This financial support relieved the mission of some of the missionaries' upkeep as well as benefitting the government by securing teachers in remote areas (Olsson, *By One Spirit*, 423).

71. Knapp, (Alaska Governor, *Report of the Governor of the Territory of Alaska to the Secretary of the Interior,* 1892, 51).
72. Sheakley, (Alaska, Governor, *Report of the Governor of Alaska to the Secretary of the Interior* 1893, 5).
73. J. Arthur Lazell, *Alaskan Apostle*, 106.
74. Almquist, *Covenant Missions in Alaska*, 74.
75. For instance, Alfred P. Swineford, (Alaska Governor, *Report of the Governor of Alaska to the Secretary of the Interior,* 1885, 13); Knapp, (Alaska Governor, *Report of the Governor of the Territory of Alaska to the Secretary of the Interior,* 1891, 496); Knapp, (Alaska Governor, *Report of the Governor of the Territory of Alaska to the Secretary of the Interior,* 1892, 57–58); Brady, (Alaska Governor, *Report of the Governor of Alaska to the Secretary of the Interior,* 1900, 34–35); Brady, (Alaska Governor, *Report of the Governor of Alaska to the Secretary of the Interior,* 1901, 50).
76. Robert Fortuine, *Chills and Fever*, 180, 191; Larson, "Our Alaska Mission," 167.
77. Almquist, *Covenant Missions in Alaska*, 72–73.
78. Fortuine, *Chills and Fever*, 195.
79. Ibid., 180.
80. Johnson, "Yakutat, 15 March 1905, Alaska-Missionen," 67; Johnson, "Missionen i Yakutat, Alaska," 52; Johnson, "Albin Johnsons missionsrapport från Yakutat," 36.
81. Johnson, "Missionen i Yakutat, Alaskamissionen," 76.
82. Dietz, *Mad Rush for Gold in Frozen North*, 60. Johnson reportedly held a prayer service for the gold seekers, and they sang *Nearer My God to Thee*. "The missionary was a poor singer," Dietz (63) remarked, admitting that the visitors did not do any better. The singing "must have been wretchedly poor," as he recalled, but it was so heartfelt that "I thought the noise we produced was the most exquisitely sweet music that I ever heard. I have certainly never since heard anything sung that contained such genuine realism and feeling."
83. Covenant Ministers' Record Duplicate, in Johnson, Ministerial Records.
84. Johnson, "Missionsrapport från Yakutat," 37.
85. Johnson, "Albin Johnsons missionsrapport från Yakutat," 57.
86. Almquist, *Covenant Missions in Alaska*, 132; a handwritten obituary in the Albin Johnson Ministerial Records states that Johnson returned from Yakutat "broken in health."
87. Covenant Ministers' Record Duplicate, in Johnson, Ministerial Records.
88. Covenant Ministers' Record Duplicate, Application for Pension, in Johnson, Ministerial Records.
89. Obituary, Mrs. Albin Johnson, in Johnson, Ministerial Records.
90. Obituary, Albin Johnson, in Johnson, Ministerial Records.
91. Johnson, "Missionsrapport från Yakutat," 33, 34.
92. Johnson, "Yakutat, 15 March 1905, Alaska-Missionen," 66.
93. De Laguna, *Under Mount Saint Elias*, 207. The Yakutat believed that lost or drowned individuals turned into Land Otter Men. Even in the mid-twentieth century, many Yakutat Tlingit were still afraid of the land otter for this reason (ibid., 38).

94. Ernest S. Burch, Jr., "The Inupiat and the Christianization of Arctic Alaska."
95. Leland Carlson, in his history of the controversy (*An Alaskan Gold Mine*), acknowledged numerous ambiguities and altruistic motives on the part of Covenant executive board members, but clearly condemned avaricious and duplicitous actions by the executive board, leaving David Nyvall standing as the most steadfastly honorable character in the saga.
96. Almquist, *Covenant Missions in Alaska*, 55, 134.
97. Evangelical Church of Alaska website, accessed 26 May 2013, http://www.eccak.org/eccak-churches.html; http://www.covchurch.org/who-we-are/structure/conferences/alaska.
98. Elmer E. Rasmuson, *Banking on Alaska*, vol. 2, 5–6; Edward A. Rasmuson, Letter to the Reverend John Peterson; Terrence M. Cole and Elmer E. Rasmuson, *Banking on Alaska*, vol. 1,101–102. Johnson returned to Yakutat to assist for a year in 1906–1907, while Mrs. Johnson remained with the children in Chicago.
99. Harlan Updegraff, Letter to Reverend E. G. Hjerpe. The government would no longer pay a teaching salary to the only missionary in the village. According to Almquist (*Covenant Missions in Alaska*, 60–61), many people continued to serve both roles, but they were paid as either one or the other.
100. E. A. Rasmuson, Letter to the Reverend John Peterson. Jenny's salary was eliminated and his raised after they were married.
101. Cole and Rasmuson, *Banking on Alaska*, vol. 1, 106–107.
102. Ibid., 110.
103. E. A. Rasmuson, Letter to the Reverend John Peterson.
104. Ibid.
105. E. E. Rasmuson, *Banking on Alaska*, vol. 2, 48, 57, 310.
106. Elmer E. Rasmuson Obituary, Rasmuson Foundation website, accessed 8 May 2012, http://www.rasmuson.org/index.php?switch=viewpage&pageid=29.
107. E. E. Rasmuson, *Banking on Alaska*, vol. 2, 106.

Albin Johnson. Courtesy of Covenant Archives and Historical Library, North Park University, Chicago, Illinois.

Foreword

"Seventeen Years in Alaska," which is now sent by the author to our mission people, does not claim to be an exhaustive depiction of Alaska, this American land of the midnight sun, or its people, customs, and traditions, but rather it is principally a depiction of what the author himself has experienced as a missionary during the pioneer era. As such, he has come in close contact with the people, come to know them not only in their religious thinking, but even in their everyday life. He recounts what he has experienced, seen, and heard simply and graphically, as only one who has lived many years among them and taken part in both their joys and their sorrows can do. Certain episodes are serious, others comical. The contents are relatively variable and provide a better insight into the mission work in Alaska than we have thus far had. At the same time that the account evokes appreciation of the great changes that the mission work has accomplished, it should spur greater commitment to this so long neglected people. May it therefore be well circulated and in this way further the mission's holy purpose.

The Author's Foreword

Ever since I was a missionary in Alaska, I have nurtured the thought deep in my heart of publishing a book on experiences and memories that I have carried with me all these years.

Now I have brought this idea to reality and therefore leave to the public this candid depiction.

I have taken the material from memory and experiences as well as from journal entries and other writings on Alaska.

The writer does not claim to place his work in the same class as those of other renowned writers on this land, but these are my experiences as I have recorded them.

Fully aware of the shortcomings inherent in my work, I hope, all the same, that the book will serve and be of interest to readers, as well as to some extent bring joy and light, and further God's purpose on earth.

Chicago, Ill., 31 July 1924.
ALBIN JOHNSON.

Mount Saint Elias
HUBBARD GLACIER
Disenchantment Bay
MALASPINA GLACIER
Russell Fjord
Old Village
Monti Bay
Yakutat
Situk River
GULF OF ALASKA
0
50 m
0
50 km

ALASKA
ARCTIC CIRCLE
Ft. Yukon
Rampart
Circle
Yukon River
Nome
Golovin
Nulato
Fairbanks
Eagle
Unalakleet
Tanana River
CANADA
St. Michael
Iditarod
Holy Cross
Kuskokwim River
Susitna River
Anchorage
Valdez
Cordova
Seward
Skagway
Yakutat
Juneau
Sitka
Kodiak
Ketchikan
Alsek River
CANADA — BRITISH COLUMBIA
UNITED STATES — ALASKA
Dry Bay

I

THE CHILDHOOD HOME

The childhood years are a delightful and beautiful time, and our childhood memories follow us throughout life. This time is also a foundational time for our eternal well-being. It is a blessing to be able to forget the darkness and difficulties of various sorts that we have experienced, but it is pleasant to carry with us the pearls and roses that we have gathered along the way. In particular, the spiritual impressions—if we had a home where such were imparted—are priceless.

When the writer's thoughts return to these happy childhood times and I meditate over childhood memories, my mind is afire and my heart warms with childhood's happy days. It would be difficult to find a more simple and full life than I had. I thank God for my parents and home, where I ran so happily and played my childish games, benefitting from loving care. The free country life was a school. The fresh air and simple ways were wholesome.

It was not in a red painted cottage with white trim that my cradle stood, but rather in a secluded farm that bore the old-fashioned name Svedjefall in Härje Parish in Västergötland, where the writer first saw the light of day.[1] My father was Johan Larson; my mother was Lovisa Larson.[2] They owned a farm, which they operated so that it could provide us sustenance. The brood was rather large—a chain of ten—but three died at an early age; thus the chain then consisted of seven, in which the writer was the last link.

My parents struggled and worked hard to sustain the home and provide for all of these children with healthy appetites. We learned to work at an early age. Simple customs and a simple lifestyle were the rule in our home. Sundays were devoted to God. Usually we listened as Father read from the Bible or another book, and we went to church.

The Svedjefall farm was situated in Västergötland's forested highland, and a more naturally beautiful place would be hard to find. Birch groves, high mountains, hills, valleys, creeks, lakes, and beautiful spruce and fir forests alternated with meadows in the landscape in this part of Västergötland. It is impossible to forget all of this. However much I had to help with all sorts of work, I had just as much time to play with my siblings, and it was not hard to find interesting and entertaining things to do in such a rich environment. We played in the forests, swam, fished, picked flowers, and enjoyed ourselves to the fullest. My home was not wealthy. Our food was simple, but when we had bread, herring, and mashed potatoes, we thought it was a feast. At the age of eleven or twelve, when all of my older siblings had moved out, I was home and went to school and helped my parents with all sorts of chores.

Of the childhood events that have remained in my memory, this should be mentioned: I was to tend a herd of sheep for a neighbor, and then I learned the lesson that it was difficult work to be a sheepherder because the sheep ran all about, and I was told to keep them together and count them and see that I did not lose any. I tried with great zeal to fulfill my assignment. Weeping and worrying, I carried out my venture in sheep herding. Here in the forest, among birches and greenery and junipers, I thought of God and prayed to Him. During my childhood the great revivals were in full bloom in our district. I had the privilege of accompanying my parents to hear Jönköping's colporteurs and other preachers of the Word. In the message they preached were spirit and life, and God's word took hold in my heart and in my mind. As I guarded the sheep, the thought occurred to me that the Lord could make me a skilled preacher or missionary when I grew up. I used to climb up on tree stumps and stones and preach to the sheep in the forest. Experience has taught me that God heard my prayer.

Among the memories I carry with me there is one in particular that I would like to recount. My oldest sister, Josephina, had been working for a faithful cleric, from whom she heard the living God's word. She had also heard the renowned spiritual singer Oscar Ahnfeldt and learned to sing some of his songs. She came home to visit and sang:

> "Dare you, boldly, believe that Jesus did all for you
> The only begotten Son, He did, the only begotten Son, He did."

She also sang:

> "During the day at my work
> I think of You."

I thought that this was the most beautiful message that I had heard. I joined in the song, and then my sister said to me: "Go on, sing, Albin, God's angels love to listen." This sister has gone home to join in the heavenly song, but I was happy for what she then sang, for to sing of Jesus was precious for me, and is now more precious than ever before.

My father was a self-taught Schartau follower.[3] During the free-church revival era he became completely converted and joyous in his belief in God. But it took longer for my dear mother to accept Jesus. However, before she passed away, she found peace with God, and I nourish the hope that we will meet in Jesus' home.

During my childhood I also had the privilege of attending elementary and folk school.[4] I had a very strict teacher, an enemy of the free-religious movement that swept through Härje Parish. But then I began confirmation school and had the privilege and joy of studying with a pastor who was a believer. That was a happy and precious time. This pastor sought, most of all, to bring us completely to Jesus. I shall long remember the moments we spent in the rectory and hearing this man's warm testimony about Jesus, the savior of sinners. I believe it was on Pentecost that we were confirmed in the Swedish state church in Velinge. Oh, what important and lovely memories from that time!

After I was confirmed, I left my childhood home and traveled, seeking my luck on my own. Because I had siblings in Jönköping, I set out in that direction. The farewell from home and my parents was emotional. My dear mother supplied me with what she had. A little bundle was my earthly inheritance, but the most cherished was my parents' and God's blessing, and when we have God's blessing, we are rich. Saying farewell was difficult. Father and Mother told me that I should take God with me, for then all would go well.

I found work in Jönköping.[5] During the first part of my stay there it was as though I was pulled in two directions. Sin's temptations and seductions were strong, but many of God's children who believed in Jesus were here in this town. I followed them and heard God's word and joined the choral group, and thus came the happiest moment in my life. An older brother asked me one evening if I wanted to give myself to Jesus. Moved as I was, I answered with a determined "Yes." In prayer to God, I poured out my heart and belief in Jesus. What a turn my life took! Jesus now became so cherished and dear, and I found it wonderful to be among God's children.

Jönköping's Christian youth group at that time held warm and uplifting meetings in town, which I attended and valued highly. It was educational for me and a preparation for my life's calling. We young believers went to the edges of town where, together with an older Christian, we held meetings in homes. I have lovely memories from that time. The Word was not sown in vain.

After several years' work in Jönköping I traveled to Ångermanland, where I stayed awhile. Although I held a management position in a store, I found time to hold Sunday school classes and work among Norrland's people. Up there I began preaching throughout the Ådal villages.[6]

I now felt a deep need of more knowledge and guidance and familiarity with God's word and therefore sought and won acceptance into the Swedish

Mission Organization's Mission School in Kristinehamn.[7] I spent nearly three years there. Then I received from the Organization in Sweden a call to be their missionary in Alaska. I accepted the call with great joy, for I was prepared to go wherever the Master wanted to send me.

II

THE JOURNEY TO ALASKA

The Mission Organization had called upon the renowned missionary August Anderson, who was then a pastor in Värmland, to proceed to Alaska.[8] Everything was prepared for the great and memorable missionary induction ceremony in Kristinehamn's mission house. It was a large gathering of friends of the mission, teachers, and students in the mission house that evening. Doctor Ekman led the whole ceremony. It was an emotional and memorable moment. Many words of comfort and Bible verses were lavished upon us.

The same evening that we were approved as missionaries, we commenced our journey to Alaska. One day in Gothenburg to arrange for tickets, etc., and we were on board one of the Wilson Line's old steamers. The weathered rock formations in the archipelago disappeared quickly from our sight, and we were soon gently rocked to sleep by the ocean's waves. No exit pass went with us; we had to make our way as best we could, and it went excellently.[9]

It was pleasing to the eye to see the first glimpse of America's coast. Now we were in New York. Great happiness prevailed among all when the big steamer *Alaska* landed in the calm harbor.[10] How were we to find our way in this city? Well, the missionary pastor Professor Erickson, who was our guide while we stayed there, met us. But we did not dare stay here long; rather, we set out again through America to San Francisco. Here we were given a couple of weeks to study English.

My goal was Yakutat in southern Alaska. August Anderson would accompany missionary Axel E. Karlson to Unalakleet, in northern Alaska. Missionary A. Lydell, who had to leave Yakutat owing to illness, met me in Portland. We then traveled together to Seattle, Washington. There we waited for the boat that would depart northward. Boat connections between Seattle and Alaska were not much to count on at that time. Steamers went as far north as Sitka and Juneau, and usually through the Inside Passage. I found a tourist steamer by the name *E. D. Elder* that served Sitka and Juneau. With trust in the Lord I boarded that boat. It was very pleasant to be among only Americans.

My English was now put to the test. I found the American friendliness and helpfulness very agreeable.

To travel along Alaska's coast through the Inside Passage is very pleasant. The scenery is enchantingly beautiful. The route winds among countless islands. The fjords extend far in between the mountains; high and magnificent glaciers shine forth; rivers and waterfalls rush down into deep valleys. The great spruce and cedar forests fill the air with their fresh aroma. The country is very sparsely populated. Here and there a village or fisherman's home can be seen.

The boats at that time carried many tourists. Our boat made multiple stops, where we could go ashore. It was interesting for everyone to see the villages and Indians. At Muir Glacier the boat stopped, and the passengers had an opportunity to climb on it.[11]

After a week's sailing we landed in Sitka and Juneau. This was the tour's destination. But my goal was Yakutat, which lies 260 miles north of Sitka. I stayed in Juneau a couple of days with a Presbyterian missionary and became acquainted with missionary work among the Tlingit people. But I had to reach the journey's destination, and how was I to arrive there? This became a burning question. Well, "luck comes and luck goes, but luck follows those God loves."[12] A sailboat was heading that way, and I was given an opportunity to come along. It cost twenty dollars, and together with fifteen gold seekers we started our journey, which took us twenty days. Through storm and calm the small craft rocked forward. If everything had gone well, we would have been in Yakutat in two days. I have made many difficult journeys, but this was among the most worrisome. First we had tailwinds, and it went at the wildest speed. We were heading out on the open sea on one of the most challenging sailing routes in the world. Before we set out we were going to take in wood and water. When we had pulled in to a harbor on a cape that projected out into the ocean, we anchored the little schooner. The sailors rowed into shore to gather wood and fill the water barrels. Others gathered clams to bring as fish bait, for the boat was also going out fishing.

It was clearly spring on the land where we moored. Nature was green and inviting. When we were anchored there, I became restless. One day I asked the captain for a rowboat to row to land, because I wanted to pray and do my meditations in the forest. The sea was like a mirror. The birds soared on light wings over the bay. I received a boat and set out with all my might. I had not rowed more than about eight or nine hundred feet from the schooner when completely unexpectedly a great whale suddenly appeared just ahead of the boat. The roar of the water pillar he sent up, and being so near this sea monster, nearly scared me to death. If I had rowed briskly before, it was now a battle to avoid coming in contact with the whale and being swallowed up like Jonah.

When I had calmed down a bit, I thanked God that the whale did not appear under my boat, for then my grave would have been in the ocean's waves. The Lord protected me from danger. In the forest I had an unforgettable moment with God. The air from the tight spruce forest and sea were truly refreshing. However beautiful the nature and fresh the air, it was nevertheless clear that the land was desolate and uninhabited: wild lands and wild water.

After a couple of days' rest, we set out in our craft on the wild sea, sailing with tailwinds. The captain then said: "If everything goes well, we will be in Yakutat in two days." But we experienced something else. After a half night's sailing we encountered a furious storm that seemed as though it would break the vessel into pieces. The sail had to be reefed; one man bound himself to the helm and then raised a little sail; it resembled a stretched handkerchief, and the boat had to drift out with the wind, out on the roaring and angry sea toward Japan. When the sea had calmed, all the sails were raised and the craft was steered toward land. We then sailed for three days before the peaks of the tall Alaska mountains could be discerned. I prayed to God for good weather for landing in Yakutat. During the strong storm that we endured, I even saw Catholics and gold seekers, who were fellow passengers, cross themselves and call out to their God.

God heard our prayers. It became calm and still. We now lay by Malaspina Glacier, right in front of the great, stately mountain Saint Elias, which rises high into the sky with its eternally snow-covered crown, 19,000 feet high. It was now very calm after the storm, so we cast out hooks and caught great, splendid cod. I understood that we were in a rich fishing area, where whites had not yet had time to snatch or destroy the fish. We now had to hurry to cook the fresh fish, and because we had all been seasick and unable to eat, it tasted good.

Once again we were to experience a storm, but it did not last as long. In any case, it did not take long before we were in sight of Yakutat Bay. While the wind was calm, we ventured to take the schooner into the bay. We worked with all our might and succeeded in rowing the big sailing vessel into the harbor.

At midnight on the 11th of May 1889, we dropped anchor. If I ever felt grateful to the Lord, it was now. God had brought me to my destination. We were all tired, and therefore planned to rest as soon as we had anchored. But the savages came like swarms of mosquitoes and climbed up on the boat,[13] speaking in their curious language: "Tlinket, Häete, Nowu, Häete Nowu; Häete kunse, häete kunse." "Give us brandy, give us brandy—give us tobacco, give us tobacco." They did not receive brandy, but they did get tobacco. These people struck me as so curious—copper colored, dirty, poorly clothed. Only the savages' appearance met the eye. The terrible evil, sin, craving's miserable dark mission, had been among the people before the missionaries and had sown weeds on the garden plots of the heart.

It was a strange feeling I now experienced. Is this Yakutat? What beautiful nature! The mission station was here, but where was it located? I was now to look up missionary Henrikson, for he was there before me.

We lay down to rest for a couple of hours, for it was midnight. Early in the morning I arose, and having come up to the deck, I glanced around in the archipelago. It was a beautiful bay, with a multitude of islands and inviting, beautiful shores. In the distance were tall mountains, the tallest I had seen. Here and there among the peaks the white glaciers shown forth. Our boat lay tied in front of an Indian village.

I was eager to learn where the mission station was and therefore took a rowboat and rowed ashore, steering the boat so that it landed right in front of the village. But now there was a commotion among the dogs. Several scores met me with raucous barking. Therefore I did not dare land, but rowed to the schooner again, where I learned that they were not dangerous.[14] Therefore I tried again and pulled ashore, in spite of all the protests from the angry dogs. But after some searching, I did not find the white missionary's little cottage. Where could it be? We were in Yakutat, after all. After scanning the bay, I saw another Indian village directly across from where I was, and further down, at the edge of the spruce forest, I saw a small house. There I saw a column of smoke rising from the cottage that indicated that someone lived there. That must be it, I thought, and immediately steered the boat there. As I hit the shore with the boat, a thin, mild-looking man with a sincere and happy face stood there. I greeted him: "Good morning! Is this missionary K. Henrikson?" The answer was "Yes." "I am missionary Albin Johnson from Sweden, sent by the Swedish Evangelical Mission Organization to be your assistant." "Welcome, welcome," responded Henrikson. We entered the little cottage. I thought that it was a cordial meeting, and entering the primitive little cottage felt moving. We were to be bearers of light here among these people—the Tlingit. Brother Henrikson had been alone all winter after Brother A. Lydell had to leave owing to illness. Brother Henrikson and I were soon amicably conversing, working, planning, and so on. We had to set to work immediately. The second day I was there, Henrikson suggested that we should go hunting wildlife to have some fresh meat to eat. This pleased me greatly.

The landscape was unfamiliar to both of us, and we were eager to learn to know it. It was spring, and most of the Natives were up near the mountain hunting seal in the pack ice. This land was truly a paradise for the savages, because the land and the sea and the streams were teeming with animals and fish. I had never seen anything like it.

The mission station owned a big rowboat. We took it and rowed into an unfamiliar bay of the sea, and here a great archipelago called Anchor Creek appeared before our eyes. We were to hunt here. Brother Henrikson had a good rifle, and he was an old and experienced hunter, too.

We crept into an alcove near a large tidal plateau. There we saw a swarm of wild geese singing their wild tones. Suddenly they took flight with a horrible shriek, flying over us where we lay in wait. They flew high, but Brother Henrikson made an attempt and sent a shot at them. One was hit, and it fell to the ground. Now we had fresh meat for several days, for the wild goose was big, fat, and gorgeous.

We were now satisfied and rowed home. That was how fetching fresh meat was done in Alaska at that time. Not surprisingly, the savages loved this land. Here the white man had not yet encroached on his territory, in contrast to today, when Alaska's lands are inundated with whites, and Native complaints fall on deaf ears.

III

MISSION WORKS' FOUNDING

Preparatory work in Yakutat was done by the missionaries A. Lydell and K. Henrikson. Above all, this must be acknowledged and appreciated. Now I had to familiarize myself with the work. The Indians came and visited me, but their language seemed impossible to learn. Such strange throat sounds!

We planned to build a school, church, and children's home, as well as educating the children and holding gatherings. The work was difficult and heavy, for we needed wooden boards, and we could not obtain them from a sawmill as in the States. We transported logs, sawed, planed boards, framed and built, did the finishing work, built chairs, tables, beds, and so on.

I used half the day for various chores and during the other half I taught a class of children. We felt our obligation great and our strength limited, but God was with us. That was the reason that we made progress. I believed that the mission's work should operate with a long preparatory educational effort, but we learned that God's power is great in the weak and that the Lord's light allows Him to find His way into heathens' hearts and do what no other power can.

A FIRST FRUIT'S SHEAF

One of the very first to be brought to Jesus was a lame man, a cripple like a biblical Mephibosheth. He was a despised person about whom no one cared. He was often mocked, scorned, and abused by the people, but those whom people discard Jesus lifts up and assists.

Satshrook was the man's name. He had heard of the white priest "Nocke-ned." We could easily imagine how joyful the man became—crippled as he was—when he dared to visit the mission station. Along the beach he walked at a slow pace. When he came near the mission station, our big dog took off after him, barking with all his might. The cripple was completely terrified and threw himself on the ground and screamed as loud as he could, as if his life were in danger.

We called the dog back and invited Satshrook in, and one could not have imagined a dirtier and more miserable creature than this cripple. But inside this exterior rough skin glowed a warm heart. He was eager to hear what we said and accepted the instruction about Jesus and believed in the savior we proclaimed. He was poorly equipped intellectually, but he learned both to speak English and to read. He came to love the mission and the missionaries and was true to them until his death. Satshrook became friends with all the missionaries who came to Yakutat. Early each day he made his way up to the mission. He learned to sing several songs. Though he did not understand the words, he hummed along just the same.

Everyone cared for him, and one missionary, Selma Peterson, had a cabin built for the man high up on a hill with a window facing the mission station. Satshrook lived here in peace and quiet, and when he needed something, it was not far to the missionaries. Often, often we heard him singing, and it was uplifting to hear him. And on account of this cripple, these words of Jesus came to me: "if these become silent, the stones will cry out."[15] Memories of this man often come to me; I hear his song and see his happy expression. However poor, miserable, lame, and despised of people, he had cast in his lot with the beautiful, and a lovely inheritance will come to him. Satshrook is no longer here. When he accepted baptism, he was given the name Ned Swanson. Ned passed on, believing in his Savior, several years ago. He has gone to meet his God.

THE FIRST CHRISTMAS IN ALASKA

The wild Indian was not familiar with the great celebration Christmas. It was with the missionaries' arrival that it became known. The greatest of all celebrations that brings joy, light, and a festive atmosphere to large and small is Christmas. It is also the Savior's desire that we should carry the joy of Christmas to all the peoples of the world, for it befits all, and is for everyone.

It was in spring 1889 that I arrived in Yakutat. Through the following summer we energetically built and prepared for the coming winter. In particular we set a goal of having a room ready so that we could hold large gatherings. Missionary K. J. Henrikson worked from morning to night. In the mornings I held school, and in the afternoons we joined hands in building, furnishing, finishing desks, etc., and when the cold, windy fall arrived, we had a room, a hall, ready to gather in, so that we could celebrate Christmas in Alaska. The following will provide a view of just how we carried out the Christmas celebration.

The Natives in the Yakutat region then knew little or nothing of Christmas and its great significance. All days were alike for them. They had little awareness of Sunday, so it was not recognized either. The Tlingit people used to engage eagerly in a great number of pagan feasts and events, and these were their only solemn and celebratory traditions, but everything bore the mark of rawness, horror, and the darkest heathendom, leaving only grief and worry in their darkened hearts. Thus, these northerners were in the Lord's thoughts, and they would now learn to celebrate the memory of Jesus' birth. Christmas was approaching, so Brother Henrikson and I wanted to make it as festive as possible. Several months before Christmas we had related that Christians always celebrate Christmas on the 25th of December every year, and they therefore waited and asked time after time: How soon is it Christmas? They wanted it to come soon, for they thought the wait was long.

Finally Christmas Eve arrived, and there was a great rush at the mission station. Brother Henrikson took his rifle and ax and rowed to a bay in the Pacific Ocean named Anchor Creek to shoot ducks for the Christmas dinner and to fetch a large Christmas tree. The undersigned had to stay home and tend to Martha's concerns, for we had not yet had time to bring up any female missionaries.[16] Of everything that had to be done, the question was how we would come by any decorations for the Christmas tree. We had lights, and we made candies. But more was needed to make the tree gay. Well, in the village there were dyes that the women used to color spruce roots and grass for the baskets they created. We used these to color paper red, blue, and green for the tree, and thus the tree was ready, and we all thought it was beautiful with its modest trim. It was time to gather the people together, for it was already 5:00 p.m. Darkness had fallen, the sea howled, heavy snow fell, and a sharp wind swept along the beach, whipping the area. A sturdy Native boy named Gust Sannie was given the task of notifying folks. He took a large frying pan and rushed up a hill near the village, and with a wooden club he beat the signal on the frying pan. The summons was heard throughout the village, and soon there was a chain of people from the village to the mission station, walking up to the Lord's house. The little unpretentious church was soon full of Tlingit people. They were not so refined, clean, or elegant, but they were happy to see the candles burning in the tree. We heard them exclaim "Klehurtsch Ucke—Sle-kotse schra" (It's very beautiful and oh, this is great). "Gunal—chease gunal—chease" (Thank you so much, thank you so much!). A spirit of reverence overtook the people. We sang, prayed, and preached the gospel, and they were deeply moved. They prayed to God, confessed their sins, and rejoiced with us that Jesus had come to the world to save lost sons and daughters. The gathering lasted until late in the evening. But the people were not enticed by spiritual food for the soul alone; they also received buns and candies, which also contributed to increasing their gratitude. We parted that Christmas Eve very happy and grateful to merciful God. The Natives did not forget the impression that was made, that we understood, for some time after Christmas an old man came to us and said: "Hurry up and arrange for Christmas again, for it was so nice that we want to have it often." He thought we could arrange Christmas when it suited us. Blessed ignorance! Since then Christmas has been celebrated in Yakutat year after year to the rather great pleasure and cheer of the poor people. The mission work has progressed. They now have a fuller program that is conducted by the people with a greater understanding of God and His goodness. It has now become a custom among the younger people in Yakutat to gather early on Christmas morning and sing in Christmas. It is *julotta.*[17] They go from house to house, awakening the sleeping with Christmas carols. I will never forget how wonderful it was to be awakened by songs of Jesus in the quiet, dreary, cold Alaska night by those who earlier were wild pagans, who had been warmed by Jesus' love and whose voices had been tuned for heaven. Yes, wonderful and treasured memories, and You, eternal God, shall have the glory for everything for all time and eternity.

VICTORY SPOILS FROM THE MISSION FIELD IN ALASKA

It was during the winter of 1890 on the little Khantaak Island in southern Alaska that a great feast among the Indians or the so-called Tlingit tribe was to take place.[18] The cold wind from the north and west blew, and a thick layer of snow had fallen. The great sea that surrounded the island on all sides pounded the outer shores with its powerful surfs and the murmuring, deafening, thundering noise created a terribly wild impression overall. The island is not large, only a couple miles long and close to the mainland, but not far from Hubbert Glacier, which is one of the world's wonders. On this island was a large Indian village, with its customarily built, cold, and poorly constructed houses. In the chief's house, the largest, preparations for the potlatch were under way. Wood for the fire, and various sorts of food, such as fish and great amounts of seal oil, as well as blankets and calico fabric, which were to be given away at the "potlatch," were brought in. Natives from distant villages had been invited to the feast. People from as far away as the distant Stick Indian village in Dry Bay had come.[19] It was a cold winter evening before the actual feast had begun; the undersigned and a missionary, K. J. Henrikson, made a little journey from our station in Yakutat to the island to visit the people of the village. We were heartily welcomed by Chief Jana-Shoo. He said: "I am glad that you whites have come here to teach the people; my people know nothing, understand nothing, and are like dogs."

We told him of how we would open schools, arrange a home for children, and build a church, where we would teach the people to know God and mankind's savior Jesus Christ. This pleased the chief, and the news spread among those gathered that we would take the children into a well-built house, and that they would receive proper clothing and as good food as the whites ate. There was a family that had an orphan girl by the name of Datt-sherke, who had been brought there by relatives and was dirty and tattered, as well as so cold that she was shivering. An older Indian woman was caring for her, and when the girl, who was about six years old, saw us missionaries, she ran to us and sat with us, announcing that she wanted to come to the mission home. We took her to the mission and Datt-sherke, or Esther as we called her, grew up in the home, learned to know Jesus, learned household work and went to school, where she even learned to speak and write English and became a nice little girl, a victory spoil for the missionaries in Alaska and a saved soul for God's kingdom.[20]

"Every calm breeze from the sea
Brings us new offers
of pagans who begin
to turn themselves toward God."[21]

"THE CRIERS" IN ALASKA

During the winter of 1890 an unusual phenomenon occurred in our work, just as we were fully engaged with preaching and prayer meetings, home visits, and conversation. Interest, which had flared through the cross's simple testimony, had effected a great longing and awakened life's most important question among the Tlingit people: What should we do so that we might be blessed? I never would have thought that the Word would have had such a powerful effect on a people who had so little knowledge that we had been able to share with them so far. I believed that we would first instruct the heathens for a fairly long time, but heavenly knowledge is accessible to all, under all circumstances.

In my youth I heard of "criers" in Småland, who fell into a trance and spoke to the people.[22] It was an awakening, a message to the people. Large groups gathered to hear them, and it was obvious that it was God's work among the weak souls to whom He was devoted. Now I myself was able to witness this, and out in the heathen field. The second winter we were in Yakutat we seemed to be in a great rush. The daily duties were to hold meetings and day school, make home visits, and have conversations, as well as to accomplish a great amount of practical work. People streamed in to church and heard the testimony about Jesus, the savior of sinners.

One bleak winter Sunday a messenger arrived at the church with strange news. Missionary K. J. Henrikson and I were resting awhile in the afternoon. While we conversed about this and that, a Native named Jeme Ka-kaashra came with an urgent report. This youngster was much valued by us and served occasionally as an interpreter during our meetings. He was one of the first fruits of our endeavors.[23] He was a big man with a good head on his shoulders. He informed us of much and told us how the people responded to the message. Now we understood that Ka-kaashra was on a special errand, and he tried to clarify for us that on the little island Khantaak, where there was still an Indian village with large old houses where many lived, a wonderful event had occurred, which frightened and stirred up the whole clan. The story spread like wildfire from man to man. No one had seen or heard the likes of it. What could it be? More than one person so wondered, and the question engrossed everyone.

A boy had visited our school and church, but he was reserved by nature. He had inexplicably fallen into a slumber, in broad daylight, and while he was in this condition, a sort of trance, he was preaching to the people. At least this was what Jeme Ka-kaashra said. He described the situation so captivatingly and urged us to go with him over to the island to see and hear the youngster, whom we had named Albert. We wasted no time in following him in our rowboat over a bay three or four miles to get there. Upon our arrival in the village, we stepped into a large house. Here our eyes met a large gathering of Indians, sitting quiet and still. Far at the front was a beautiful blanket spread on the floor, on which the youngster lay as if sleeping, speaking in a moderate voice for a long while to a man who sat by his side. Then the man translated it for all in a strong and clear voice as well as explained what the sleeping one said. His speech made a strong impression on all those gathered. It was a wonderful occurrence. I had heard of the so-called criers in Sweden during the Great Awakening and wondered whether this really was something similar. The Lord has many ways to carry His work forward, and this was without a doubt one way in these dark times. I felt that it was lovely to see these rays of light from the eternal sun break through to the people in this wonderful way.

Albert spoke for a long time after we entered the house, but awakened after an hour's talk and sat quietly and peacefully, apparently a little weak and tired. He did not know what he had said, but spoke of having seen lovely heavenly scenes of angels and glory. But what did the youngster say in his trance? Well, he urged the people to give themselves to Jesus, to escape to Him and be saved. As the Indians now lived, they were lost in their sins. They had great, blood-red sins. Now missionaries had come with an offer from Jesus

Christ, who had the power to save them and show them the way to heaven. Jesus will soon come. He can come at any time, and if we are not saved, we will not be able to follow Him into His house. Convert ye to the Lord! This was, in short, this wonderful voice in these dark times.[24] After such a meeting there was usually a meeting afterwards with prayer and calls to the Lord for salvation, and they led such a meeting themselves. Yes, this was wonderful, and we missionaries found it supremely gratifying.

Two young girls visited our school and often came to our church together with their parents. They fell into trances in the village located near the mission station. And if the first attraction awakened wonder, questions, and activity, this occurrence awakened even greater consternation and folk said: "Oh how wonderful, how wonderful!" What could this be?

One evening shortly after Albert's slumber these girls had fallen into a trance and firmly lectured the people. Among what they said was this: "Ask the missionaries to let us spend some time at the mission station, for our people live in dark, dark sins. It is such a sinful village." We promised them that they could come. They came and received a room. The first evening they went to bed calmly and tranquilly. During the night we heard a loud noise. What was going on? Well, the girls had fallen into a trance and spoke. A couple of Native boys who were at the mission heard what the girls said: "Run over to the village and say to the Indians that they should come at once to the mission, for there was something they wanted to tell them." It was not long before the whole mission building was full of amazed and curious people. The most mysterious in this incident was that they called out the names of one and another, commanding that they should come forth to the sleeping ones and confess their sins. Some went forth willingly and confessed. Then they were calm, while others, whom they also named and called forth, but who sort of hesitated and did not want to confess their sins, became completely wild, so that strong men could hardly control them. They writhed and flung their arms about violently, so that the people were frightened. The girls commanded them to confess their sins, and then they did so. One after another confessed openly serious, horrible, dark sins, and then they prayed to Jesus, that He might forgive the sins. And as soon as those whom the girls called by name came near, they were calm.

Furthermore, there were many others, both men and women, who fell into trances, and this went on a whole winter. At times it was in the Tlingit people's homes. One evening I visited the village. A young man had fallen into a trance and the people were greatly excited. A prayer meeting followed, and the whole group in the house prayed, greatly moved and rapturous. It was as if they literally stormed the throne of mercy. I nearly lost my composure and I beseeched God that we missionaries might be capable of leading the people rightly. Our sermons in church were well attended during this time, and the congregation was large. There was enthusiasm, with confession of sins and of faith. Many times when we preached, the people fell to the floor and fell in a trance. We then had to stop preaching and listen to them and pray with them. These were revival meetings in the greatest sense, and mercy and the Spirit's power revealed itself among rough heathens.

A dark stretch in the movement also came. It was one of the sleeping preachers who spoke against us in reproach, partly raising petty issues, and then we protested, quoting God's word. Then they complied with us and what we told them was God's word. Through this movement we believe that victory has been won for God, and on that great day the Tlingit Indian criers shall also present their victory spoils.

IV

A DARK CHAPTER

Among many heathen people, in conjunction with idol worship, the so-called magic men or witches made use of monstrous and very repugnant religious practices.[25] This was also the case with the Tlingit people, among whom such practices were done by Indian doctors (shamans), or as the people called them: "Ersh-t" (exorcist is the right name, in my judgment). They were tattered, their clothing soiled, as though they had been dipped in seal oil, foul smelling, and long haired, a braid dragging several feet after them as they moved forward. How had they grown it so long? Well, one could clearly see that it had not grown so long, but had been lengthened with loose hair, which they fastened with soil so that it should look as though it had grown, and in this way it would give the people the impression of a magical power or ability over the evil spirits and in driving out illness.

The stance they took among the people was selfish, arrogant, self-important, hateful, holding the people in a sort of fear and deepest darkness. One could say that they were the devil's special representatives. If someone was ill, the shaman was sent for to investigate the reason for the illness. The patient was laid on the floor on a skin or blanket. The "shaman" came forth now clothed in a blanket with a long pole in his hand. Now a great commotion began with utterances of "hocus-pocus" and the shaman running around the sick person, emitting the most horrible howls. Occasionally one of the people was judged to be the source of the illness. Such a person therefore had to be punished and be martyred or killed. Anyone could be met with such a verdict from the nasty shaman.

After such a "cure" from the magic man, healing was to occur in the sick person, and if someone got well—for it happens that sick people get well—the people sank deeper in their superstition and darkness. And then the sick person's relatives had to pay many blankets to the magic man.

Epidemic illnesses often ravaged the villages in Alaska. And when death harvested many, gloom and depression prevailed. In particular this was the case before Christ's light had enlightened the people. In the past, people used to turn to magic men in their distress. One of these would then go about among the people and cut or clip snippets of the sick person's clothing, after which the shaman fastened them to a long cord and with a stone for an anchor sunk it in the sea, and in this way the people believed that illnesses ceased.

In this context I would like to tell a true troll story. When Brother Henrikson and I on one occasion were out and set a fishing line in the bay to catch a halibut, one of those magic strings fastened in the fishing line, which we had to cut apart to free the line from the spell, so we could have luck and

Shaman at Yakutat, 1886–1890. Alaska State Library, Edward DeGroff Photograph Collection, P91-71.

of course fish. We now had a good laugh, mixed with a prayer to God for light and salvation for these people.

PROFESSOR DAVID NYVALL'S LETTER TO MELLANDER

In a letter to Professor A. Mellander inserted into *Missionären*, Professor Nyvall describes the Indians' character in the following way:[26]

> Naturally the natives interested me most. They are a people who inspire hope. To see these Indians with shovel and ax clear roads and build a railroad through the wilderness was encouraging. And from Governor Brady down, it was the common judgment of all with whom I spoke that the Indians are excellent workers, better than the whites who come up here. Yet they do not labor for wages unless they have no other alternative. It is the plain truth and they know it themselves and say it, that they managed just as well before with their seal catch and their fish. The Indians in southern Alaska have never suffered from scarcity. They have an overabundance of game and fish. It is even less the case that they hire themselves out because they prefer this work to hunting and fishing. The latter is still their favorite occupation. They are so civilized that they work solely for the cash that it brings in. These Indians are fully Americanized, at least in terms of valuing earning money most of all. Actually, this greed has become excessive and has become a characteristic that significantly obstructs the development of true and noble Christianity. It is a fact that the Indian willingly takes and unwillingly gives. He can hardly help it. He has been raised this way. He is accustomed to this. And a rather important part of the missionaries' duties is to elevate the Christian Indians to be a better example in this part. I am happy that our missionaries are fully aware of this duty today. Much more could be said on this topic. But it would be too detailed for a letter. What I actually meant to emphasize was that the Indians in southern Alaska are fairly affluent, have many opportunities for earnings, and there is no shortage of rich people with much money in the bank.
>
> With regard to their education and culture, it is almost exclusively what the mission's influence has given them. It is a fact that the Indians in southern Alaska in general could be divided into two large classes: good Indians, who have come under the mission's influence, and bad Indians, who have not been moved by

this influence. I do not believe that it would be an exaggeration in the least to say that whenever one meets a good Indian, well clothed, hard working, and intelligent to talk with, that he bears the mission's mark and seal. Not all of these are Christian. And thus, the Indians' relationship with Christianity is somewhat curious. Christianity for them means, as it should, everything that is good. They have no conception that one can be good and not a Christian, and even less that one can be a Christian and yet evil. 'A good Indian' is therefore well near synonymous with a Christian.

In conjunction with this stands a relationship that must be well understood to appreciate fully the difficulties that missionaries encounter in their work. The Indian is and will be an Indian, even as a Christian. He cannot cut himself off from his roots that bind him to his heritage. The whole tribe is so unified that it is impossible to have an effect on one without affecting all. It would be infinitely easier to lift one or two or a whole dozen up to a very high level, if that were possible, than to lift the whole tribe ever so little. The former would also be an effort that would be more noticeable. But that cannot happen. And what would it actually tell us? It would deprive the mission work of all its living connection and all living consequence. It would mean constantly beginning anew with each individual who was to be evangelized, and only if he happened to be isolated from every possibility of influence by his own people. Every converted Indian would then be a greenhouse plant, unsuited for normal relationships, an artificial product, not for the market as much as for the museum. Such work would be visible and as such gratifying. But it would be hopeless.

That the Indian remains an Indian is demonstrated in a terrible way in his weakness for certain temptations. Drinking and living on the edge are too deeply ingrained in his nature to be eradicated in a day or in a generation. There are few reformed Indians who do not need to be protected like children from the temptation to drink. There are few Indian women who truly have reached the level of marital fidelity. For the temptation to drink, alas, how easily they fall. And with the firewater in him, even the best Indian is in the blink of an eye transformed into a fury, ready to commit murder. I have often heard of this. But now I have experienced it at closer range. Two of my most attentive listeners Sunday morning in Yakutat, both good Indians, were deluded to drink Sunday night, while the steamer *Excelsior* came in, by a couple of whites with no conscience, and they immediately fell into a wild fist fight. This influence of ungodly whites on Indians is the most evil of all evil. It is the worst for the poor women who seem completely to lack the ability to say no to these white scoundrels who ruin them. And some of these scoundrels have names that are known nationally.

Yet, there are exceptions who manifest what the gospel can do, among whom the seed bears fruit with patience. I shook more than one brown hand whose firm handshake, together with a secure, certain look was a silent, but inexpressibly well spoken, testimony to the peace and power that conquer. Praise the Lord![27]

V

A MAGIC MAN HEARS THE GOSPEL

My dear wife often used to visit the Tlingit people in the village. In a wretched cabin she one day found an old magic man, ragged and dirty with his long terrible hair, sitting beside the fire warming himself. She entered into conversation with the man, spoke with him of Jesus' love, and invited him to come to our church; she asked him first to clip off his long ugly hair and wash himself clean and to come to the mission station so that he could be given whole, clean clothing. After a couple of days the man actually came, bathed and with cut hair. It was almost more than Mrs. Johnson dared to believe. But he received a full suit of clean clothing. Later he also came to church and heard a sermon of God's word.

The superstitious belief system among the people had begun through the gospel to be undermined. For the light escapes the dark, praise the Lord, and then even magic men are moved.

PRACTICAL WORK

A missionary should be a "Jack of all trades," for his is an edifying and teaching work. We built a church, schoolhouse, children's home, dwelling house, and more. We even taught the Natives all sorts of trades and work. Missionary Henrikson was a practical man and contributed to this creditable effort. One undertaking especially gave the mission a great upswing and was greatly valued. Their old dwelling houses were in very bad shape. We were promised by the Organization we could buy and build a steam sawmill. We carried this out with much work and trouble. When it was operating and they saw how we could saw boards, there was much joy among the people. They tore down their old houses and built new ones. With great joy and song and dance they came to fetch timber from the sawmill. Some stayed there all day and watched, astonished by the machinery, repeatedly exclaiming: "Klehutshe, kletkow, slekotse kletkow!"—"What amazing things white men do!"

One day when we were occupied with sawing, we had a log that was too big to saw into boards with the circle saw that we had, so we decided to blow it into two parts. We therefore drilled several deep holes, in which we set gunpowder and fuses, which we lit. The log lay in the water during this process. All at once the shots fired with a deafening sound. The log split straight down the middle, but imagine our astonishment when the Natives came with their boats and asked "Vase-vunne, vase-vunne?" (What's going on, what's going on?) "Did the saw blow up?" No, no, we replied, and showed them the big split log. Now there was joy and laughter and once again, "Slekotse kletkow!" (Aren't the white missionaries amazing!)

Many interesting events are associated with the practical work we performed. Among the skills we tried to teach them was even farming, but we found that the Indians had no interest in it. We cleared the ground, planted potatoes, root vegetables, carrots, beans, etc. They grew rather well, and thereby demonstrated that it was possible to grow many things for sustenance. We even made a flower garden, and many sorts of flowers grew well. However, it was not so easy to protect them, for when the Natives came, they walked right up through the flowers, and potato plants were pulled up early to see whether there was anything in the ground.

To prepare bread was for them unknown. When they bought flour, they mixed it together with water and boiled it like "doughnuts" in seal oil.

They came and asked us to help them bake bread. Our women missionaries taught them how. A man came once to learn this marvel. His wife came along, but she sat and watched. Everything had gone well, and it was a matter of waiting for the rising process. Now it so happened that a steamer came into the bay, and they abandoned the dough and the bread and ran and found their canoe and went out to the steamer. The steamer's arrival was an interesting event for those who lived so isolated. The next day they came to complete their bread baking, but by then the missionaries had baked it for them.

AN OLD LEGEND

A government representative who for several years had resided in Sitka and thereby made himself well acquainted with the people up there told the following, which I will reproduce from "back home."

He did not believe, he says, that there was a single legend left among this peculiar and lighthearted people that he had not heard of, or that there remained in the area a place of interest that he had not visited. But one lovely summer day, when an old Native named Klanaut rowed him and his interpreter in a canoe around on the completely calm bay along the jagged beaches, they came to a place where they understood, based on the Native's behavior, that a heretofore unknown mystery lay hidden. The old Alaska man would not hear of putting them ashore at this place, but the more they sensed his resistance, the more curious they were, for they became certain that in the forest up there on the hill there must be an object that the Natives considered holy. They finally came ashore, found their way through the thick forest, and, when they came up on the hill, they saw one of the Native's "Kaht Tah ah Kah ye tea," or a little house for the dead, rather carefully built of fairly large logs. Beside the little cabin lay a large canoe and inside it a smaller one—both old, decayed, and overgrown with moss. When they had entered the little house through the roof, they saw two objects that had been wrapped in linen several times, which they immediately understood to be the remains of two human beings. They lay there side by side, the one much smaller than the other, and by each one lay a box with many household items and hunting equipment. Metinoff—as the interpreter was called—was daring enough to unwrap the smaller bundle, and when he had taken off a couple of layers of bark and finally opened the other wrapping, they saw, to their amazement, a little skeleton of a white girl. Her long, blond hair had not been damaged by decay, but shone in the sun rays that found their way through the roof of the little cabin. Great was both men's astonishment, and it was even greater when they found inside the carefully wrapped shroud a little New Testament, on the title page of which they read: "Bainbridge & Co., Printers, London, 1788." They stood quietly a long while, wondering how this little wanderer had come there and how she had come to rest there in the wilderness. Reverently and tenderly they laid the testament back and rewrapped the weak, fragile bones, and after they repaired the cabin's roof, they hurried down to the canoe to try to get some information from the Native there on this secret. Klanaut was at first very sullen, but when he learned that they had not plundered the grave and taken something with them, as curiosity seekers normally do, his mood brightened. It was some time, however, before he was willing to tell them something of what he knew. But after he had sat awhile and thoughtfully gazed out over the sea, he suddenly said: "I will retell the story as my people have told it for me." And here follows now his story, which the above-named official, Arthur Villiers, after careful investigation found was completely true. We reproduce it here as he reported it, thereby following the Native's vivid description as closely as possible:

A long time ago, long, long back in time, before any large ships or white men had come to our coasts, when the mission men and mission women all slept and there was not a single Christian siwash in Alaska,[28] there lived in Sitka—not this Sitka, but old Sitka, seven miles south—a shaman, a high medicine man who was very great and powerful and who was feared by every chief and lineage. He had done many peculiar and wonderful things, and even while he was rather cruel and feared no one, his reputation had spread along the whole coastline and even up the rivers among the inland lineages, so that his word was law and no one dared disobey him. He was a very big and strong man and could recognize a witch by merely looking at her. He killed all magic men and witches that he could find, and he found many because there were a large number of men, women, and children whom he did not like, and there was more room for him in this world if he sent them over to the other, and thus he used to pass much time in tormenting witches until they died. He was a very ugly shaman. When he was young, he had singlehandedly fought with a bear in the forest and had killed him, but the bear had clawed out one of his eyes and ripped off a part of his nose and one side of his face, so that when it healed, he looked like a worse evil spirit than any of those he could speak of. Sometimes he used to go to a potlatch—which as we know is a feast where the chief or master of the house, who hosts, gives away many presents—and if he was not satisfied with the gifts he received, he used to immediately accuse someone in the chief's family or the chief himself of being bewitched and thus forced the gathered guests to lead them out to death or torture.

These tortures were something terrible—so horrible sometimes that the Natives used to walk away and leave him alone with his victims, coming back a long time thereafter to find him mutilating their dead bodies.

The evil spirit grew in him year after year, and all the lineages feared his presence—for his arrival meant certain death for someone among their people. But at the same time, they believed him, otherwise they would have killed him. One woman, whose husband and three children he had tormented and killed on different occasions, followed him to his house with this intent. She waited until he had fallen asleep and then crept near him, raising a club to strike him in the head, but a great black raven flew in through the door and pulled his long hair so that he quickly awakened and grabbed the woman and tied her up and gave her to his dogs as feed. He himself told of this, and it was believed, for the woman never came back to deny it.

One time a great feast was held in Sitka, and Tlingit people came there from far away, and there were a large number of them. The Chilkat people arrived with great pomp. They were very cruel and warlike, and from time immemorial they had forced the Tlingit people who lived inland to pay taxes before they let them come down to the sea. They came with many large warships and all of their clan chiefs came also. With the great *tyee*'s family was a white girl with golden hair, perhaps ten years old.[29] She was as beautiful to look at as a salmonberry flower, and the Chilkat people were very friendly and attentive to her. They said that she had come to them from the sea three winters ago and that she had been with them ever since. She had learned to speak the Tlingit language, and her small fingers were very quick in making baskets and weaving the chamois' long hair into blankets. She had a talisman that she observed very closely, and she told stories for them, of which she said her talisman had informed her. These stories were different from all those they had heard before, and they thought that they were all lies and nonsense. I understand now that her talisman was a book that missionaries speak from when they teach us to be good. Well, the girl was given an honorable position at the feast, and the great shaman from Sitka sat across from her and eyed her cruelly with his one eye. But she was not afraid of him nor of anyone else, and she sang a few sorrowful songs in a language that none of the Tlingit people understood. Now, after two or three days of celebrating and potlatching, the Chilkat people prepared to leave, and it was the last day of the feast. Then suddenly, the shaman accused the little white girl of being a witch and demanded that she be bound and handed over to him. For a time the Chilkat people refused, but the shaman was wearing his death mask and was so terrifying in his wrath that they were frightened—brave men that they were—and they went their way, leaving the little white girl crying bitterly and begging them to take her with them. Shortly after they had departed, she took her little book, which the people then called a talisman, and began to look at it very closely; and she did that until they bound her hands and feet and turned her over to the shaman. And he bore her to the beach and lay her, bound as she was, in his canoe and rowed away.

Through all this the little girl had been very quiet and calm, but her big blue eyes had a distant, longing look, as if she saw a beautiful land somewhere or watched for the arrival of someone she loved. Many of them in Sitka were very sad for her sake, but their great fear of the shaman and their superstitious beliefs in his power over the invisible mysteries hindered them from resisting him or trying to help the child to avoid the terrible fate that awaited her. When his canoe had disappeared from their sight, a strong but softhearted woman raised her arm toward heaven, made a prayerful movement, and then ran away and hid in her cabin. Four nights and four days passed, and just at evening time the shaman came back alone. He was very cocky and off-putting, and if anyone dared mention the little girl, he displayed such a terrible sternness that they were all happy to be silent about her. But he behaved so peculiarly. He took from his own cabin all of his beautiful dance costumes and fine blankets, and he bought from one of my relatives a blanket made of snow-white ermine, and he gathered together the good and nice things that he could find and took them away in his boat and laid them down carefully there, and it was noticed that he was not as rough and mean as he usually was, for when small children stood in his way, he did not run at them and knock them down, but guided them kindly to the side. Then he stood in the water with his loaded canoe and said: "Farewell, my people!" something he had never done before. And all the people were astonished and watched him in wonder as long as they could see him. And at the same time he had a long conversation with the woman who had expressed her sorrow when he had taken the child away, and the woman went with him. He had become completely changed, his clothes were clean, and for being a shaman from Sitka, his demeanor and behavior were very friendly; and our people were struck with astonishment and wanted to go with him, but he would not allow it. And for many months the shaman and the woman were away. Then, on a warm sunny day, when the men, women, and children sat idly and gazing out toward the sea, they saw a remarkable canoe coming out from the shadow of a faraway island. It had a high mast with a cable that ran down from its top to the bow and stern of the canoe, and in the cable hung many strange flags, and at the very top, over all the others, fluttered a snow-white flag with a big red cross, and when they came nearer, they saw the shaman and the Native woman. He sat in the bow and the woman in front of him, and as they rowed, wailing over a dead person was heard. When they came near the beach, my people saw the little white girl's dead body, resting on a soft bed of deerskins, with her small hands laid over her breast and the emaciated body wrapped in the spotless ermine costume. She was very beautiful, and her long hair glistened like a salmon just caught at sea, and shone in the sunshine like threads of gold. Willing hands dragged the canoe high up on the beach, but the shaman sat as if dreaming, gazing at the dead child's expression, quiet just like her.

And my people did not speak a word, but waited with a certain dread.

Suddenly he walked carefully up on the beach, turned his scarred face toward heaven, and he spoke thus:

> My people, my family, I know today, in truth, that you are all my brothers and sisters. I was born among you; my childhood, my youth, my adulthood I have experienced among you here by the great water. I have until now lived life as a shaman from Sitka as in the old times. I have been very stern and evil, and I have lived a murderer's and liar's and thief's life. Although I have thought of myself as a brave man, I know that I have only been a cowardly wretch, and I have today brought back to you the little girl who has taught me to recognize these bitter things.
>
> She is dead, but before she died I promised her to retell the story for you, so it is not just I who speaks, but it is her lips and heart that speak through me. When she first came to us from the Chilkat people, I wished to own her, and when I took her away to my cabin in the mountains, my intentions were very evil and sinful. I know that now; then I did not know it. It is a day's travel to my home in the mountains, and shortly after I had left here, I

released her, and she came trustingly and sat at my feet in the bottom of the canoe, and lay her head on my knee and looked up in my face with eyes like a young deer's. I turned the ugly side of my face from her, so that she would not see it, but she noticed it and raised her little hand and patted it. She did not make fun of it or push it away from her, and I felt like a hunting dog, being stroked by his master. No living man or woman had ever been friendly to me before, as long as I could remember.

Then she had me tell her how my face had been so ravaged, and when I finished, she called me "courageous" and stroked the scarred place, saying: "Poor face, poor face."

I don't know how it was, but I had a pain in my heart and something came up in my throat so that I gasped for air. Then she said that she was going to tell me a story, and she told of one who was God's Son, the great *Tyee*, who created the earth and the skies, the sun, the moon, and the stars, and how this God's Son gave His own life for evil people like me and died a cruel death, so that I would not have to suffer for my own sins, and I would believe in Him. She said that He was friendly and mild just as a child, although He possessed great power and could do everything. Thereafter she fell asleep and I sat very still so as not to awaken her, and I observed her face and thought about the wonderful things that she had told me. I did not hasten to bring her to my home and I stopped rowing and let the boat rock slowly with the waves. Far from the island, where the sky meets the water, it looked to me as though the day dawned, for instead of becoming darker, it became clearer and clearer, and I could see the shine of the white seagulls as if the sun shone on them; but here, where we now stand, and along the whole mountainside, it was so black that I could not distinguish anything. I thought that this was a sign and a mystery, and I wondered if the child's God was soon to come over the west water to visit her, for she had told me that "he was clear and shining," and so I waited and watched while the child slept. Suddenly the light disappeared and a cold wind came from the sea, and I thought I heard the familiar magic voices speak, and my heart hardened, and I awakened the child quickly and pushed her from me and began to row in fury; but I had forgotten to note where we were before the light disappeared, and I did not know where the boat had drifted. I was frightened, for I had never been lost before, and I had never seen such a dark night. And while I was cruel and mean, I said to her that we were going to die, that a sea troll had pulled us toward its home, where we would be killed and eaten.[30] Then the child came and bent her knees at my feet and held up her small hands and said many words in a foreign tongue. Finally she said in the Tlingit language: "Do not be frightened, for I am with you always. This is a promise from your and my God and He will rescue us." And shortly thereafter the wings of darkness lifted and went away, and I knew where we were—not far from the place where I was to go ashore. And I pulled the boat ashore and carried the child up the steep path to my cabin in the mountains, and I could not be stern or evil toward her. She told me such wonderful stories about her God, that I was one of His children, and of a beautiful land where He waited for our arrival, and that we, by living kindly and believing in Him and doing good, would after our death here be welcomed there and never have any sorrow or suffering again.

And I had never been so happy in all my life. I brought her all the things that I valued most, and she turned my cabin in the mountains into a lovely place, and I loved her as a mother loves her child and I could have suffered everything for her sake.

One day she said to me that God called her and that she had to obey Him and leave me for a time. Then I wanted to see Him face to face and fight to be able to keep her with me, but she said to me that God was with me every day and moment, and that He could only be won with love and submissiveness; and she told me much more, until my stormy heart rested in peace. And then I saw her wither away like a flower each day, and near the end she could not walk or eat herself, and I came here after Ne-that-la, whom you all know as a kind woman. She followed me and cared for and nursed the white flower as well as she could, until the time came when God touched her heart, and it stopped.

Shortly before she left us to go to His beautiful land, she extracted a promise from us both to try to come to her and to lead as many of our people as we could to follow us. She said that she would wait for us on the other shore, and based on this promise and because I, who loved her, wanted to be with her forever, I have brought her dead body here to rest among my own people; and when I die, I wish to be laid by her side on the hill that I have chosen as my last resting place. And, oh my people, if ye will take notice and obey a piece of advice from a shaman from Sitka who has learned to love and be kind, so shall ye believe in one God alone—this child's God.

Thus he finished, and the women in the clan prepared the little body for its long rest in the "house of the dead." And they laid her book, her talisman, in her lap and they wrapped the ermine dress around her and they placed all the presents from the shaman in a box at her feet. Day after day the shaman waited alone on the hill by her body, and night after night, in storms and clear weather, he sat watch to ensure that no harm would come to it; and one morning, after a fierce storm, he did not return to the village, and when some of the people went to look for him, they found him dead, sitting by the side of the house, holding onto it securely, as if he did not want to be torn from it. And my people laid him by the girl's side and placed his canoe close by, as well as a smaller one for the child.

That is all I know.

Here Klanaut stopped talking. And I believe that there was a trembling movement in Metinoff's eyelid and in mine and a tear that wanted to slip out. I have visited the place many times since, and I think of the beautiful child and imagine her as pleasing as the lilies that sway around her last resting place, and I wonder whether the shaman found her—waiting on the "other shore."

THE TLINGIT INDIANS' CONCEPT OF GOD

The religion these northern people had was shamanistic, i.e., belief in spirits, spirit works, and good and evil spirits. They were trained in witchcraft, spirit incantations, superstition, and under their pagan condition, during long and terrible darkness, the true concept of God was nearly completely destroyed among the people.

The Tlingit people believed in a good spirit: "De-kee-ankow" (the above-living good spirit), which they believed was natural, was always available to them, and never did them any harm. Therefore worship or praying to the good spirit was never a part of their religion. However, what did take place was worship and praying or spirit incantation to the evil spirit, whom they called "De-gre-an-kow-oo" (the reigning evil spirit power), who was thought to dwell down in the earth's interior, in the dark regions. The evil one and the evil spirits were thought to be constantly against them, causing misfortune, hindering them in their hunting and fishing ventures, and possessing them when they were ill; therefore it was the shaman's task to drive away the evil with magic. These evil spirits were frightened away through howling, shouting, and noise, after which the road for the people was thought to be free of obstacles. Sin and guilt were not so clear for the Natives. However, I noticed they had a God-given law embedded in their consciences to distinguish between right and wrong. Life after this life was very unclear and dim. Many opinions were maintained. If they had lived an admirable life, they would go to the heavenly hunting grounds, but if not, they went to worse, dark places.[31]

Their creation story was essentially the following: The first creature that existed was a little seabird called a diver, which species is found along the shores of the Pacific Ocean.[32] This created first the raven, which was the actual creator of everything. First the earth, the sea, and everything except humans were created. Then the raven decided to create the human being to live and reign on earth. The raven flew, so it is told, over Alaska's seacoasts and came to a place where much driftwood had floated ashore, and in a moment man was created of driftwood and stumps. According to this creation story we men have come from driftwood or stumps. Woman was created differently and of a living animal. The raven flew south out to a bay in southern Alaska by the name of Redoubt. There is an island there, very lovely and in the form of a beehive. Here the raven came on his creation journeys, and on the same island a multitude of crows gathered, making a loud noise. Instantly the raven created women out of all the crows.

The Tlingit people's creation story falls apart into incoherent acts and different events with lost links here and there, which clearly shows the people's darkness in this respect. But a more childish or even amusing event than the one below, which is how the story goes, is hard to find in any pagan religion. The following is told:

The raven was thought of as the creationist power. He flew over the land and water and plucked up driftwood for his servants. He claimed his ancestry from a great chief's daughter. He first appeared from a bud on a tree. When the great chief's daughter drank water from the spring, she swallowed the bud, a life's seed, which in the chief's daughter caused the raven's conception. And when the raven was born, he cried for daylight to no avail. Thick darkness enveloped the whole earth. Sun, moon, and stars were all condensed in boxes and bags that hung on the wall. In the midst of the incessant screeching, during which no one could console the raven or knew what should be done for him, one of these curious boxes hanging on the wall was taken down. The raven lifted the lid, and out flew the stars and hung themselves in the sky, and in this way they were created. But the raven continued to wail. Then another box or bag was taken down from the wall and given to him. He opened the lid and out flew the moon and hung itself in the sky. But they were still having great difficulties, while the raven continued to cry loudly. There was yet another box remaining on the wall. It was taken down, and when the raven opened the lid, out flew the sun and hung itself in the sky. Hereby there was daylight, and now the raven at last was consoled, for it was sunlight that he had been wailing for the whole time.

With the opening of the light box, first a little light was let out, then the full sunlight in all its glory. The effect of the sunlight was great. Everyone was frightened; fear and trembling overtook everyone on this wonderful occasion. But what did the people do before this miracle of light was created? Well, it is told that in the darkness they were occupied with fishing a sort of ling cod—fat, small fish that were caught in the rivers in southern Alaska and are very good tasting and liked by everyone.

Then the raven was hungry and asked for food, but no one would give him anything to eat. The raven said: I will frighten them by sending the daylight over them. Now the people came to the raven, some clad in bear skin, some in fox skin, seal skin, bird skin, and so on. And as each came, the raven created bears, foxes, seals, birds, and so on.

Then the raven left on a journey again and came to a place where he stored all the water, and he opened it and let it run out, and in this way formed the seas and oceans of the world.

"WHALE KILLER FEAST"

The people held a grand feast. Whale Killer was a big chief with great abilities and many servants. These servants were snipes who were to dance at the feast. They did so with great ease and grace. All the birds were to file into the hall arranged in a train, which they did, except for one snipe that was so extraordinarily stupid that she could not march arranged in a train, but rolled in as a piece of wood.

Here the raven appeared again and asked Whale Killer how it happened that the snipes danced so nicely and easily. Whale Killer said that he had rubbed charcoal in their eyes, let all the snipes lie down in a long row, and drove a twig into their heads with a hammer, except that one of them, the stupid one, refused to take part in the process, and therefore it remained stupid and could never dance for the rest of its life.

After the dance came the banquet. Everyone was invited to it, even the fox, a creature in their sagas, but fearing that he would not be respected as a big chief and be seated in the place of honor, he did not want to come. The feast began without his presence. The raven, however, could not stay away from the feast. He dressed up in a white hat with feathers and finery. Arriving at the banquet hall the raven cried: "Where should Run-na-nolke sit?" Nobody listened or paid attention to him. So he entered the banquet hall and seated himself in the place of honor. At that moment the raven was, according to their stories, demoted, and so ends the story of him in darkness.

TOTEM POLES

Among the Alaska peoples a curious and almost unparalleled custom is that from time immemorial the various peoples and clans have carved or painted their various clan characteristics in images, partly human images, partly various animal images, such as the eagle, the bear, the wolf, the fish, or the frog, etc. Every family or clan has a unique totem, or clan symbol, by which they are known.

In many Alaska villages, outside the houses stand very tall totem poles, up to sixty feet tall, carved from huge trees in a variety of animal, fish, and human figures. These poles tell a variety of their old worship stories, both funny and sad. Like a book among the white people, these tell of events among the clans. So, for example, the frog totem is the most prestigious image, of which they feel proud.

It was said that the Tlingit people held a great feast in some village long, long ago during the raw pagan times. When the festivities were at their height, a white frog appeared among the celebrants. All of them viewed the frog as a revelation, and they decided to name themselves after this frog to commemorate the event. All of the revelers in attendance were chosen to belong to the frog clan, and subsequently they were to mark, paint, or carve a frog on all their belongings to distinguish themselves.

But how could these people save all these stories among themselves? Well, it has been accomplished by carving in wood and bone as well as painting these figures on everything possible. Also, in later years they have engaged in trade by producing every imaginable curiosity for tourists and selling their products. These are richly decorated with totem figures in bright colors, for instance bags, oars, knives, forks, baskets, etc. They have thus developed for themselves an industry and earned much income. At the same time, it has been very interesting work for them.

WEDDING IN ALASKA

Marriage relationships among the Tlingit people were very muddled when we opened the mission there. It was a large task for the missionaries to teach them Christian customs and traditions. The people lived in polygamy. Old men married young girls and young men old women. Their old customs and laws permitted it. When parents planned to marry away their daughters—this took place while they were rather young, say ten, twelve, fourteen years old—the girl was placed in a little room by herself. Only the mother could see her. Here she occupied herself with handwork, her face painted dark brown. After six weeks or three months she was taken out of this prison. The idea was that after such a cure she would be beautiful and her parents would receive a higher price for her. When she came out of imprisonment, she married, and the one who married her had to pay rather substantially to the girl's parents. The payment consisted of blankets, bear skins, seal skins, and other skins, from a hundred to four hundred blankets and a variety of skins, depending on whether a girl belonged to a higher or lower clan. The old widows often married young men, for they were poor, and the young men did not have to pay anything for them. This disorder understandably led to hate and unhappiness, quarrels and unfaithfulness. This is paganism in its most terrible form.

The Christian mission was the death knell for polygamy, and it has been almost completely eradicated. The younger generation has developed a taste for cleaner customs and traditions, and it is now scandalous for a Native to live in polygamy. They now come to the mission station to be married. So-called church weddings with their customs and traditions now take place there.

AT A FUNERAL

The Tlingit used various ways to bury their dead. The most common old practice was cremation. Important men and at times children and especially Indian daughters were not cremated but were placed in small houses specially constructed for this purpose. However, to cremate the bodies was the normal practice. A big fire was prepared and the dead was thrown on it with howling, groaning, bellowing, and crying. When the body had been cremated, the bones that remained were stored in boxes, and beautiful pieces of fabric were wound around them. Their old grave mounds were dotted with special small houses, like playhouses, in which the bones of the dead were stored. Since the mission began, the Tlingit people have learned to bury their dead like the whites, and we missionaries held sermons and talked to the people, and gave those who were believers, especially, a Christian funeral.

On the little island Khantaak an old and prominent man had died. I have now forgotten his curious name. It was late in the fall. I went together with Brother K. J. Henrikson out to the island. In a big house everything was prepared for the funeral. The deceased had been placed in the front room of the house on a high platform in a sitting position, so that it looked as though he was living. He was clothed in beautiful brightly colored wool blankets. Just beneath him were four chairs or bench seats, which were meant for the most prominent mourners. Henrikson and I were invited to sit in the middle, and to the side of us, on the right, sat the first chief, Jana-shoo, with the magic man Dettion on the left side. First a big feast took place: boiled rice, crackers, sugar, coffee, seal meat, and oil were consumed. The group of mourners was large. While they ate, the people told adventure stories from bygone times, noting especially what the deceased had accomplished in bravery, in hunting and fishing, etc. Certain acts honored the spirits of the deceased. Someone took the best food or the best clothes and threw them onto the fire, recounting as many of the names of the deceased as they could remember. They believed that the spirits of the deceased came to them on festive occasions and observed them and accepted their gifts. After such a large old-fashioned funeral the body was cremated as described above. This feast lasted for many hours. We missionaries were offered peach preserves and were spared having to consume the repulsive seal oil and what they had prepared themselves. After the funeral, the people chanted or sang in lamentation, which lasted hours and whole nights, as they wept over their deceased. Everyone cried, and everyone began at the same time on the command of the chief or magic man. After the same command everyone also stopped instantly. Thereafter they usually laughed and danced and played, and it was as if everything was to be forgotten and tucked away.

VI

A LITTLE GEOGRAPHY

At the most, but a few people have a sense of how large Alaska is. To say Alaska contains 580,107 English square miles does not give us clear enough insight, but it can be better understood if one mentions that a straight line drawn from the northernmost cape to the southernmost is as long as from Maine to Florida.[33] Alaska is as large as all the middle states and New England states added together; with Ohio, Indiana, Illinois, Wisconsin, Michigan, Kentucky, and Tennessee together; or as large as the whole United States land area east of the Mississippi River and north of Georgia and Carolina—nearly one-sixth of the area of the whole United States. Alaska could be divided into five hundred states as large as Rhode Island. The governor in Alaska has said that its area is 369,539,600 acres. The coast land with all the bays' incisions is approximately 26,000 miles long, more than the distance around the world. A single gold mine in Alaska has produced seven times more gold than the United States paid for all of Alaska. Alaska contains approximately 21,000,000 acres of coal-bearing land.[34] It cost the United States less than two cents per acre to purchase this great land area.

ALASKA'S MOUNTAINOUS LANDSCAPE

There is something enchanting, appealing, and majestic about tall mountains. In Alaska they seem to be impossible to count, with their many formations and shapes. One cannot help thinking of God when one sees these mighty giants and their eternally snow-covered peaks. They stand there like guards over mankind, and more than once I have thought of the poet Carl Boberg's hymn when I viewed these wonders of nature. He sings thus:

> "Oh Lord my God, when I in awesome wonder,
> Consider all the works Thy hands have made,
> I see the stars, I hear the rolling thunder

Thy power throughout the universe displayed;
Then sings my soul, my savior God to Thee:
How great Thou art, how great Thou art!"[35]

Mountain ranges run in all directions in Alaska and many are insurmountable, hiding in their interiors countless riches for the coming generations and the nation's development. Some peaks are very high; indeed they are the highest peaks in the States. Mount Saint Elias near our southern mission station is 19,500 feet high.[36]

One of the explorers sent by the United States, who tried to climb Saint Elias, reported to me thus when he returned with dashed hopes in this venture:[37] With the ascent up the mountain, up high the expedition came to a cluster of rather large lakes, where likely no human had ever traveled, or dared to go so far up; we encountered much life and activity in and around these lakes' shores. It was then summer, with vegetation and the beautiful free world of wild birds. The lakes swarmed with wild geese, wild swans, cranes, ducks, and other birds. They had traveled here from all parts of the country to spend the summer. Here they could be in peace from people who often plunder their nests. This is the birds' heaven or Eden. God has created everything wonderfully, who could question that? Bears, chamois, mountain goats, and other species also thrive up in the mountain regions. The Indian often treks far up to hunt them, and more than once I had the pleasure of procuring wild meat from Indians after their hunting rounds, which were very challenging and dangerous for them. The savage understands that one has to dare in order to succeed.

EARTHQUAKE AND FIRE-SPEWING MOUNTAINS

What vast powers lie hidden in our earth. Under our homes, where we live, sleep enormous fires. I had never reflected on it as much as when the earthquakes occurred in Yakutat in the winter and summer of 1899. It was an experience that we will never forget. One would think that in a mountainous land like Alaska the earth's crust would be very thick and all would be quiet and calm, but it is the opposite. The whole coastline from California north is unstable and most unstable in the vicinity of the great mountain regions of Mount Saint Elias and Mount McKinley. The whole long stretch of the Aleutian chain from Cook Inlet is more or less volcanic.

At different times of the year they come alive and erupt after having lain still for shorter or longer periods. It is estimated that there are between thirteen and twenty volcanoes in Alaska. Many of them are still active. Particularly, Illiamna near Cook Inlet, with three clearly visible craters that rise up ten to twelve thousand feet above sea level, still erupts fire, gas, smoke, and pumice. In the past twenty years large changes have taken place among the volcanoes, islands, and bays in the vicinity of Kodiak and Cook Inlet. New islands have formed, others have disappeared, and mountaintops have crumbled and fallen into the valleys, filling them with stone, ashes, and soil. One cannot trust these sleeping craters. Under and inside them awaits death—volcanoes.

It happened not so long ago on the 6th of June 1912 that from a United States postal ship passing through a fjord in the vicinity it was observed that the long ago extinguished volcano Mount Katmai was erupting massively. About sixty miles from the sea a great pillar of smoke could be seen; gas and fine lava came toward the boat at the speed of an express train. Mighty, deafening rumbling, worse than the strongest thunder or canon fire, put fear and terror in the passengers and crew on the boat. The captain steered straight out to sea in order to save the boat and its passengers. One explosion followed the other. The people wondered if the whole world had exploded. They looked toward the mountain; no mountaintop was visible there. The black cloud over the mountaintop resembled a black tub floating miles high. For two hours the stokers worked in the boat's boiler room to fire up the engine as much as possible, to move the boat at greatest speed out to sea. But the black cloud came closer and drove before it thousands of winged birds trying to escape. The whole deck filled with them. Some of them soon died from exhaustion. All at once the steamer was enveloped in the darkest cloud, which carried stone, gas, and lava. The passengers crawled into their cabins; only the crew was on deck. One could barely breathe, and everything was covered with lava, soot, and dust. The poisonous gasses had penetrated in, too. Red turned brown and all silver turned black.[38]

Earthquakes occur often in Alaska. It was in September 1899 that we witnessed a very large earthquake in Yakutat. We were sitting inside, conversing in a room after the morning sermon. It was unusually warm and calm. Suddenly the building began to shake. What's going on, who's shaking the building? Well, it's an earthquake, I said. Let's go outside. Everyone ran out while the whole earth was trembling. The whole world had the tremens like a drunk. Then we had a long series of earthquakes for several weeks. The earth cracked in many places. One island was flooded over by a tidal wave that filled it with sand, so that afterwards the tallest trees stuck up only a few inches over the sand. Another arm of the island sank and was washed away by the sea. A tidal wave rushed into a valley where there was a large forest and mowed down the forest as well as peeled the bark off the trees. The top of one mountain exploded and tumbled down into the valley, filling it with rocks. One Sunday we had to flee to a hill and camp out there for three weeks for fear of a tidal wave on the low land, where the mission station was built.[39]

One Sunday we gathered in the church for the sermon. All the Tlingit people were there. I had not planned to have a meeting that day, for the earth was so unstable, but the chief had said: "Are you afraid, Johnson? Now we must go to the church and pray to God for help." I replied: "Come to church." They came and everyone prayed to God, who has all power in heaven and on earth. And we had a prayer meeting in truth and power in the little church in Yakutat. However hard a time it was, especially for my spouse and children, who were then small, the Lord carried us through, and He always protected us.

A MOUNTAIN CLIMB

On one occasion, when I for some reason was visiting Sitka, which then was the capital city—now it is in Juneau—I did a mountain climb that I will never forget. Our objective was also to hunt deer, which were very numerous in the region.

One sunny morning—such as one sees only in Alaska—we set out in full hunting attire in the hope of climbing a mountain chain on Baranof Island. My guide was seaman and mountaineer Alfred Johnson, an old, experienced adventurer. I believe that he was from Småland. We had arrived and pitched our camp in Katlaske Bay, a beautiful bay in the Pacific Ocean with a mountain wall in the background. The following morning at sunrise we rose early and got ready. We had a difficult but interesting day ahead of us. We took off through the dense spruce forest, with rifle on the shoulder, upward, upward until we were over the high treetops, and wandered through the dwarf tree region and finally up to the mountain ridge's highest point. Here was truly a paradise of flowers in all its radiance and splendor and glory. I had never seen anything like it before. The whole mountain range was covered with countless flowers of different colors and species. As far as the eye could see the mountain ridge was thus covered. One could not imagine a more beautiful scene in nature. Like a great pilgrimage route up high on the even ridge ran this wide floral carpet of flowers; although so hidden from all mankind, it nevertheless in a certain way praised the Great Creator. Not even Solomon in all his glory was as well clothed as one of these.[40]

PROFESSOR DAVID NYVALL'S VISIT TO THE MISSION STATION, SUMMER 1903

When Professor David Nyvall visited Alaska in the summer of 1903, he wrote in "The Mission's Friend" some travel letters, of which I will transmit the following passages:

A more homey setting than our mission station in Yakutat would be hard to find. In the lee of storms and bad weather on the "good side" of a natural harbor a few miles deep and a couple of miles wide, forming a bay in the large Yakutat Bay, with forest-clad heights on three sides, lies the mission station in its vegetation and its peace like a refrain from the Psalms: "As the mountains surround Jerusalem, so the Lord surrounds His people."

My first days in Yakutat were favored—with rain and more rain. Yet I have to say that there was something unusual about this rain; so that with but modest exaggeration, I contend that one does not get wet from it. Perhaps it would be more correct to say that one did not pay it any attention. In any case, it worried us little. My only regret was that, with these clouds over us, I could not get even a glimpse of the massive icebergs that are the region's most renowned pride and in fact are the largest and most glorious in all Alaska. When Sunday arrived just as rainy or rainier, I basically gave up hope of sunshine or mountain excursions.

But it was to be otherwise. Monday dawned with a partly clear sky. And from that day on it was clearer and clearer. And just as I benefitted from the typical rainy day, I also benefitted from the most typical sunny days. I could not have encountered more glorious weather if I had ordered it especially for my objectives.

Now it was the right moment to set out for the heights to see the mountains and glaciers. We arranged it as well as we could under the circumstances. Or, more precisely, our friend Albin Johnson arranged it for us. A schooner that lay in the lagoon ("the mission lagoon," as it is called, because it is close to the station with our old saw at its shore) had offered to take us up toward Yakutat Bay twenty-five to thirty miles to Disenchantment Bay, a curious bay that juts into the land and then swings parallel with the coast southward for about sixty miles. This bay is completely full of glaciers and scenery of the most glorious nature. The name means "resolution of an enchantment."[41] And there really was something bewitching, at least from a distance, before we finally reached it and the enchantment was broken.

———

As we steered out from the edge of the island, the sunlight from the setting sun broke through toward us with an effect that drew the oars out of our hands irresistibly and extracted from us a common lengthy and deep exclamation of wonder. It was my first view of the mountain. And a more beautiful one could never meet the human eye. I shall never forget it. But how shall I fully describe what I saw and what I felt in that moment? My camera was hidden under the pile of bundles where the doctor sat. Otherwise, I would have, in violation of all principles and regulations of photography, tried the impossible, to take a "snapshot" of the scenery, the sunset, and everything. Perhaps some kind of magic would have attached it to the film. As it was, I only saw, saw and drank in, I don't know whether with my eyes or immediately with my soul, a beauty that appeared heavenly. The gates to Hesperides' garden, to Paradise itself, opened wide.[42] The horizon glowed in fire and flames around the setting sun. The light was not clear and sharp like the day's, but eternally soft and eternally colorful; a light not in the clear commanding tone of the day's solo singer, but broken in an array of tones: a choral song of light, a fading chord, taking in all harmony of the full scale, of all scales, of all keys, a major and minor in a single chord. In this light the majestic, snow-covered mountaintops raised their heads like giants, listening in reverence to a heavenly music from the opened temples of light.

A cartographer never could have found a more favorable occasion to draw from nature the sharp lines of these mountaintops, stretching in a chain hundreds of miles along the horizon. To the left the giant among them all, Saint Elias, raised its pyramid peak eighteen thousand feet in the air.[43] Somewhat to the right rose Augusta with a horizontal ridge and on the right a little round turret, reminiscent of a horse's back. Even more to the right, with a broad, blunt, cone-shaped top, Mount Cook dominated. And to the right of that stood Vancouver, with a snow top that so amazingly closely resembled the contours of a lion that we agreed to rename it the "Sleeping Lion Mountain." To its right the contours of the mountaintops were lost more and more in the shadows and dusk of nightfall.

We encountered a multitude of icebergs, most of them small, and in every conceivable shape and combination of shapes. There was one in the form of a whale that raised its shiny tail in the air and floated alongside of a boat also of the clearest ice. There floated Venus in a clam shell. There a vase of crystal clear glass floated on a wave. And all around us floated rings and ornaments of all shapes. But over all of them towered an iceberg that drew our attention as much with its huge dimensions as with its wonderful shape. The one half was a church, with steeple and windows and everything. It was so obviously a church that for an instant we actually wondered this time if our eyes deceived us. The other half was a boat. And between the church and the boat was a bridge of crystal. We rowed to it and I took a couple of "snapshots" of it. And the closer we came, the more complete was the illusion. We rowed around it. We came to a distance from it on the upper side and looked back. And the sight we then saw was enough to lift our spirits for days afterwards. The church had disappeared, but the boat remained. And instead of the dignified image of a church, an image so comical met our eyes that it should have won first prize in any contest. The church was transformed into a cow that struggled up the gangplank with an Israeli or someone else from the Middle East, perhaps an Arab, at the tail and an Eskimo, yes absolutely, a genuine Eskimo with a fur collar and all, at the horns. It was not only I who saw the phenomenon. We all saw it. And the longer we viewed it, the more clearly everything stood out. I'm sorry to say that when we rowed by our wonderful iceberg in the afternoon, even this spell was broken, and our church, boat, and everything was in ruins.

View Island was the name Albin Johnson gave to the island that was to be our Nabau.[44] Elsewhere the island has another name, though I have not heard or seen it. It was a wonderfully beautiful island, so near the right shore that the passageway between the island and the shore was like a canal or river. The flower-covered sides of the island's shores rose toward the sky. The shore on our side of the island was craggy, and we found an excellent landing place there by one of the cliffs. Thus we reached our destination. But with a sound instinct for the practical we decided to eat dinner first, and then, full and unconcerned, take a look at the glacier. We had had headwinds the whole way up. The return trip promised tailwinds and comfortable sailing, instead of slavery with the oars. We therefore prepared a temporary sail consisting of a long pole and two smaller cross poles fastened to the former, as well as a tarpaulin, fastened in all four corners to the cross poles. Everything was now in order, and with our minds at ease we were able to walk around and enjoy the benefits of our efforts.

We thus climbed over the rocks and ledges past dizzying abysses to the north side of the island, where we found ourselves a fine vantage point, and so only the viewing itself remained. Unfortunately, we were still seven to eight miles from the glacier. But even at that distance the spectacle that met our hungry eyes was "a meal for the gods," to say it slightly in pagan terms. Through the binoculars the edge of the glacier looked like a great vertical wall of crystal clear ice that filled the whole bay's width. Actually, we did not see the whole width, because a part of it was obscured by a cape that extended out from the right shore. Suddenly a huge pillar of ice plunged down into the foamy water that splashed up against the ice wall, and the cannonade that we had heard since our arrival at the bay's entrance resounded with increased strength. We observed in silence, saw, and longed for a closer view. Alas! if only we had had two weeks instead of two days, so that we could have continued the journey into the bay. For some reason the general drift of the icebergs was into the bay, not outward. Albin assured us that from time to time the bay was so filled that it was completely impossible for a boat to enter. Yet it so happened that it suited the icebergs to sail outward. What caused the apparent drift is not fully understood. The Indians claimed that the icebergs drift against both the wind and the tide, and they appeared to be inclined to ascribe a supernatural cause to this movement. This is pagan superstition, of course. I cannot say whether the observation that the icebergs drifted against the wind or the tides is accurate. We ourselves had the misfortune of having both of these powers against us, and we spared no effort at the oars in driving against them. But what oars moved the icebergs against these combined powers, *if* they defied them, I do not know. In the case that the pagan superstition of a spirit in them does not suffice, we will have to suggest some scientific superstition about magnetism and attraction and leave the mystery in safekeeping with them.[45]

ALASKA, A LAND OF GOLD

Although Alaska is a northern land with ice and snow, it is by no means a poor land. God has deposited in this land greater riches than anyone can imagine; half is not known. Alaska is only partly discovered. New gold fields are being discovered continually. In the great mountains, rivers and marshes, streams and beaches, millions are yet sleeping. Yes, the resources in many areas wait for people to claim them. The big gold discoveries in the interior, and especially in Nome, have enticed thousands and thousands of people there to seek their fortune. But not all have found it.

In Alaska by the end of 1911, in round numbers the enormous sum of $195 million was extracted. Since gold-mining work first began (in 1880), minerals worth about $206 million have been extracted.[46]

ALASKA'S CLIMATE

When one speaks of Alaska, people usually think the land is full of ice and snow, uncivilized and wild in every way, with an eternal winter of the most severe cold, and unsuited for habitation. This impression is still so ingrained in people that it is impossible to convince them of the truth. Alaska, in this respect, is completely different from public perceptions. The varied climate conditions are wonderful and remarkable. The whole coastline from Seattle up to the Aleutian Islands has a temperate climate. Winter is very mild, occasionally like the fall on the west coast,[47] rain in some places and here and there heavy precipitation, but with rain weather temperatures. On the Pacific coast islands it is sometimes so mild that one can succeed in overwintering cattle and horses without having to give them anything else to eat but what they can forage on the ground. The reason for this is the warm Japanese stream that runs along Alaska's west coast and warms the coastline. On occasion, real "Chinook" winds arrived in March. The wind was so burning hot that one could not sit in its sweep for the sake of the heat.[48] Then the snow would melt rapidly, and it felt like being in warm Kansas.

Fur clothing is not used nowadays by the Natives in southern Alaska. Sometimes when there were heavy snowfalls, I saw the Natives go out into the forest and chop wood without clothing on the upper part of the body. They could do it because the winter is so mild. An old deeply rooted belief with the people is that by defying storms and showing that they are not afraid of bad weather, they can counteract storms, snowfall, and foul weather. As an example, I can relate that at the mission station in Yakutat, which lies at the 60th parallel, i.e., the same latitude as Stockholm in Sweden, the lowest temperature that has been recorded is 10 to 11 degrees Fahrenheit. It must be said that Yakutat lies on a lowland that juts out into the ocean and receives an abundant share of the warm ocean currents. At the mountain twenty-five miles from there, the cold is more than twice as severe. In northern Alaska, as well as in the interior, by the glaciers, the cold is very severe and the climate very dry. In the interior, a temperature of 45 or 50 degrees below zero Fahrenheit, even to 75 degrees below zero, is not unusual, so one could not say that Yakutat is the dwelling place of ice and snow and cold.

In southern Alaska rainfall is very high. It is said that Sitka, Juneau, Yakutat, and other places have the greatest precipitation in the world. Precipitation measures sixty-five to ninety inches and some years up to two hundred inches.[49] The humidity is so high and so penetrating that everything becomes moldy, even houses with heating.

As a result of this, the vegetation flourishes. Trees, grass, flowers, and bushes of all sorts grow profusely. Moss grows like a long beard down from the tall spruces and cedars. Even so the maddening and difficult "death club" grows there, causing the forest wanderer difficulties with its poisonous thorns. I have also found linnea there as well as lingonberry bushes, etc.[50]

WILD BERRIES

How fantastically God has created everything from the smallest to the largest! A great many wild berries grow in Alaska, and in many places in abundance. Never has greater profusion in this respect been seen. The so-called salmonberries—perhaps the correct name is wild raspberries—grow in great abundance. I could walk into the forest and in half an hour pick a whole bucket full. Some of them are very big, red, juicy, and good tasting. When they are ripe, everyone picks and eats them. These berries are the first to ripen in the summer. The wild strawberries ripen in July. These latter grow on the great plains along the sea in the Mount Saint Elias region. Both whites and Tlingit people pick these, and they taste sweeter than those cultivated in the States. In August the blueberries ripen. These grow on large bushes and very profusely. They are tart and very tasty, as well as healthy. We could pick thousands of barrels of them in the forests near Yakutat. Furthermore, "dewberries," cloudberries, and a type of berry that grows up in the mountains called "soapberries" are found there. The people highly value these because they can be dried and pressed into patties and stored and used on festive occasions. What is remarkable about these berries is that when they are mixed with water and processed, the mix becomes like soap lather with a reddish color. The Tlingit people call it "Indian ice cream." A small patty commands a high price. At the big potlatch feasts the finest dishes are made of these berries. One takes a big bowl and dissolves in it a piece of one of these patties. Two young men with just their hands and arms work the mass until the foam stands high in the bowl, with its beautiful rose-red pulp, after which the bowl is borne around among the celebrating crowd. Then people crowd in to grab a handful with bare hands. This way everyone gets to taste the dish as long as it lasts, and it goes like hotcakes. These berries are not good tasting, but bitter, but they are eaten more for tradition and their beauty's sake.

VII

HUNTING AND FISHING IN ALASKA

Hunting and fishing are popular activities as well as wholesome and healthy recreation. Many engage in them as their profession. This is the case with the people in Alaska. Fishing is easily learned, so that both small and large can participate in it. Few countries are as rich in fish and wildlife as Alaska. From time immemorial the forests up here have teemed with wild animals. In streams, rivers, fjords, and lakes fish play in unbelievable abundance. This, together with much else, causes the Natives of Alaska to love their land as highly as any other people on earth love theirs, and they are especially happy when they can pack their belongings and travel in their canoes out to hunt and fish. In their easy-to-row canoes they glide forward, nearly at the speed of a steamship, despite both storm and cold. Everything wild that crosses the hunter's path falls to the hunter's bullet; useful animal or not, it makes no difference, for he is out on a hunt and is overcome with an irresistible desire to shoot.

And the fish! Out to the wild ocean the people go, where halibut, cod, walrus, and shark play. But the most fun for Alaska's friends of sport hunting is probably the seal hunt. Out on the icebergs the seals play in large flocks, and they are shot there in the hundreds, to the great joy of all. In the late summer the salmon arrive, and this is a busy time for Alaska's people. They catch salmon in great numbers along all the streams and rivers. The Native is skillful at catching the large, strong salmon with a spear. He has also learned to use the net and the seine. Salmon fishing is, next to the seal hunt, the Natives' foremost source of nourishment. They have built fishing huts almost everywhere, and whole families cross back and forth among these, staying a couple of days at each place while they catch and smoke fish. When they get tired of fishing, the men go out to hunt bear. It is an adventuresome game that requires courage, strength, and accuracy, for Alaska's large bears are nothing to joke around with. But for men in Alaska this is a matter of honor, for a man's reputation will suffer if he cannot drop a bear. Many hundreds of these colossal beasts are shot every year. Even whites have recognized the advantages of hunting and the abundance of fish in Alaska. To give a sense of the great wealth of salmon in Alaska, for example, the various canneries in Alaska preserved no less than 2,690,000 cases of salmon during the year 1902. Now that's what I call fishing! Where in the world is there something comparable? When the salmon arrive, from fifteen to twenty thousand people engage in salmon fishing. Those who preserve the fish are the Chinese, and they're skilled at it. But all sorts of people fish. Foremost, without a doubt, rank Alaska's Natives.

For us missionaries hunting and fishing were exhilarating recreation. When we grew tired of the monotonous life up there, it was a good and invigorating change of scenery for us to set out hunting or fishing. Early one morning missionary Henrikson and I shot no fewer than twenty wild geese. Another time I was out salmon fishing. We had set out a net in the lake, when the salmon came in from the ocean in large schools. We stood in the river, in shallow water, awaiting their arrival. Then a great splash was heard. "The salmon are coming! The salmon are coming!" was shouted from every direction. I stood and watched with great interest the fish's movements, and suddenly it occurred to me to kick up the salmon on the dry land. It was easy in the shallow water where we stood, and in its eagerness to follow its course, the fish did not turn back, and I easily kicked up a whole multitude of them. Yes, sometimes a person can fish like that in Alaska. In the company of Natives, it is quite pleasant to go out and fish like this. They are accustomed to all discomforts, used to the land and circumstances, tolerant of the rain, cold, snow, and storms. One also has on these journeys the utmost opportunities of catching them in a reverent mood. They are eager to hear of God, and it appears that their hearts open up more than usual on such occasions, when one is with them during their daily pursuits and adventures. If one then takes advantage of the moment and boldly casts out an evangelical seine, one has the best chance of a good catch.

Although the Tlingit Indian has lived an ignorant life over the past centuries, he has also manifested great skillfulness in carrying out certain practical work. He manufactures his own tools, appropriate for the work he does. The Indian woman has from time immemorial braided a type of complex artistic basket of spruce roots and blades of grass and colored them with dye of their own invention, taken from the plant kingdom. These baskets are sold to the tourists for a high price, and for their own use, they store berries and water in them. The men make very practical spears for spearing salmon and seals. And for catching the big halibut in the ocean they make a sort of fishhook that only this fish can reach. The finest tools, though, are their crossbows, with which they hunt the valuable sea otter. These furbearing animals are very timid and shy. The use of rifles has scared them away permanently. They were hunted in the icebergs' most isolated places. Nowadays they cannot be found, for the steamers and the whites' rifles have scared them away, people say. The sea otters were the Yakutat Indians' greatest source of income in the past.

Thirty-five years ago a sea otter skin was worth from one to five hundred dollars. Today, if they can be found, they are worth several thousand dollars. Millionaires use them for fur garments. The government has protected them for many years now. They are the finest and most expensive of furs in the whole world.

The young boys practice fishing and shooting with a bow and arrow from early childhood. They can be seen walking about shooting birds.

The Yakutat Indian constructs very substantial and practical canoes. They are known all over Alaska for their agility and ease in paddling; they float like a swan on water. They are not heavy and can be carried and dragged up and down from streams and rivers. They are easily conveyed over the tidewater's muddy flats without risk of being carried away by the incoming tidewaters. They make canoes of three sorts: war canoes, family canoes, and two-man canoes. Big beautiful trees grow in Alaska: spruce, aspen, and cedar. Most of the canoes, including the smaller canoes, are made from spruce. The Indians make their own tools for constructing them, namely an adze, a bent knife, and a regular ax. A large branch-free fir is felled, after which the canoe is formed and hollowed out with the adze from a twelve- to fourteen-foot log. When the canoe is nearly ready, it must go through the following steam process: the canoe is filled with water; many stones are heated and cast into the water, so that it boils and steams and softens up the canoe, after which it is easily broadened and shaped. It usually takes an Indian a month to construct a smaller canoe, and it usually lasts for three years, if it is well cared for. They cover their canoes with blankets on sunny days so that they will not crack. The great war canoes are usually made of large red cedar trees and are large enough to carry twenty-five men. They travel in them long distances along the seacoast. The red as well as the yellow cedar grows densely in southern Alaska and they are very valuable. The yellow cedar is sought after for finer work for boxes, chests, and so forth. It is prohibited to export it to the States. Thus people circumvent the law by sending large boxes to the States with other things in them, and then later using the boards.

The strange thing about this cedar is its pleasant smell. When it is used for heating houses, the unusually pleasant aroma fills the home. Moreover, it contains a heat factor that compares with the Swedish birch. The Natives make curiosities of this sort of wood and sell them to the whites.

On their hunting and fishing excursions the Indians are very cheerful, telling all sorts of stories and relating everything they have heard and seen,

Tlingit curio vendors at Yakutat, 1903. Library of Congress Prints and Photographs Division, Miles Brothers collection, LC-USZ62-118067, LOT 3965.

old and new. A great many of the stories are invented. I'll relate one such here, because it depicts the Natives' enthusiasm and curiosity at the arrival in Alaska of steamers from the States. Probably a white person made it up. It is said that a good Indian had come up to heaven, the new city Jerusalem, and was transported by the angel Gabriel through the pearly gates to heaven's golden streets. Everything was so beautiful and wonderful and surpassed everything that he had heard and seen. But when they were going to start walking on the golden streets, a strong call was heard from the earth: "Steamship, steamship coming!" He ran away from the angel and back to the earth again to meet the steamship. Curiosity in meeting the arriving boats is very high among these northern dwellers. The story depicts it rather ironically, but it holds a certain truth.

In school, among the children, we learned how deeply attached they are to hunting and fishing and related activities. They talk about it constantly. The children in a class at the day school were asked by the teacher one day which book was the most important and most read of all the books in the world. They had by now advanced a bit on the road to knowledge. They replied: "The Bible and Montgomery Ward's catalogue." These books are highly regarded in Alaska, and that the former stands high is an honor, recognition of the mission up there. It would be nice if it could be said of all countries, communities, and people that the Bible is the most read book of all books; that this book is the best of all can be confirmed by thousands and thousands who have learned to know it.

A BEAR STORY

To hunt bears is dangerous and adventurous in every way, and very interesting, as well. It was spring and nature had awakened anew out of its long slumber. It was sunny and beautiful weather, and the savage was eager to hunt and fish. Seals and bears could now be taken. It was tempting for the savage. A message with bad news arrived during these days. The second chief, George Naa-kaa-nee, came and related a story, but it was at first difficult for us to understand him, for he could not speak English, and we did not understand his Tlingit. Eventually the mystery was solved. One of the men who had gone out to hunt bear had been bitten and mauled. It had happened like this: Two men had shot and injured a big brown bear. Running after him in the wilderness, one of them ran right into the bear. Injured and angry as it was, it grabbed the hunter, mauled and bit him, and battered him very badly. His friend ran somewhat back, before he turned around and killed the bear. Here came the sorrow and distress. The news spread quickly among the people. In great haste the injured man was brought back in a large war canoe home to the village on Khantaak Island and was placed in one of the largest Indian houses.

There was no doctor in Yakutat, but the people trusted the missionaries. We were therefore consulted, and with medicines in our bag we boarded the transport to the village to help them and sew up the wounds and bind the bleeding. But imagine our astonishment when we saw the women sew up the wounds with sewing needles and black thread. We helped as best as we could and were allowed. We cleaned the wounds with carbolic acid blended with water. After we prayed to God, we left the wounded in God's hands. The people sat around the patient and the atmosphere was glum. They showed us missionaries much gratitude for what we were able to do. We had weak hope of the man's recovery. But a miracle took place all the same. After a rather long period of rest, he recovered fully and dared to venture out on several other bear hunts. This man left himself in God's care, was baptized, and joined the congregation.

But how did it go with his adventuresome hunting partner? Well, he had to pay his dues. He had displayed cowardice and did not stand by his friend, but ran away. For this he was judged by their law to forfeit all his worldly goods. They took his good rifle, and worst of all, he also lost his wife. They took her from him. They intended that he was to begin life anew.

THE MAN WHO SHOT MANY BEARS

I believe it was in the fall of 1891 when a large, strong Native was going out hunting and would be gone for several months. On such journeys the whole family usually went along. Here and there in the wilderness were small Indian huts on the lakes and rivers, where they lived on such occasions. Partly they fished, partly they hunted, and the women made baskets and prepared the skins, as well as smoked the salmon or other fish. The above-mentioned man had attended our meetings and learned to love God and His word. When everything was ready and he was to leave in his large canoe, he came to the mission station and asked the following: "Johnson, Too-oos-cee-koo. Dee-kee-an-kaa-oo Shrooke!" (I want to have a Bible!). "But you cannot read," I responded. He said: "That means nothing. I know that this book is God's word, and I am now going out on a dangerous journey, and if I have it, the book will remind me of God and what I have heard of Him." I gave him a Bible, thanks to the mission friends in San Francisco, who sent us Bibles. He accepted it with joy, kept it well, and carried this esteemed treasure with him. It received the place of honor in the canoe, as well as in the cabin. The man was away a fairly long time. Eventually he came home to the village again and soon visited the mission station and displayed his joy, relating that he had been well blessed, for "I have had great success," he said. "I have brought down many, many bears and got many wild animals, and this all has happened because God was with me, and I have had His word with me."

AN ADVENTURESOME SEAL HUNT

About six miles from the mission station at Yakutat, on a spit, there are large boulders against which the ocean's waves always crash. Brother Henrikson and I once rowed there to hunt. A passageway runs through the archipelago. A small strip of land holds the great open sea from heaving up its huge surges. The land and the bays there are called Anchor Creek. The Russian Church had a mission station there in earlier times, but it was destroyed by the Tlingit, and all the missionaries were killed. Afterward no light burned there until the Swedish Mission Organization opened its mission in Yakutat.[51] The remains of the burned mission station are clearly visible. Otherwise everything is overgrown with grass, bushes, and forest. We traveled there partly by foot, following the shore. We began a hike in the woods while we watched for seals to climb up on the rock formations. This forest was very dense with unusually tall and straight spruce. We saw a multitude of golden eagles glide up to the tall spruce. Soon we had our sights on one. A shot rang out and down fell an eagle that was shot in the wing. I took a large stake and gave the bird a death blow. The stake was rotten and broke. The eagle came against me in the greatest wrath, but one more shot and he was dead.

Up on the rocks lay a multitude of seals, basking in the evening's sunshine. We fired several shots and killed a few of them. But how were we going to get a hold of them in the huge swells? The surf was as high as houses. Brother Henrikson tried to swim out there, but it was impossible. The next day Brother Henrikson rowed out there and then he found the seals tossed up on the land. Brother Henrikson transported the seals home, and thus the Natives had food and seal oil, which they like so much. The Natives praised us, because they thought that we almost surpassed them in hunting seal, without having to go out to the icebergs where they can be found in abundance.

THE TLINGIT'S YEARLY POTLATCH (ANNUAL FEAST)

The Indians held a feast yearly in the late fall, when they returned home from hunting and fishing. They fish salmon until freeze-up in the rivers and lakes. The salmon go up and deposit their eggs, and remain to die, if they are not taken. Among the Indians a large family dries and smokes approximately two to three thousand salmon. They have small houses built here and there,

Yakutat Natives at the great potlatch at Sitka in 1904. Courtesy Sitka National Historical Park, SITK 3770.

Yakutat potlatch dancers at Sitka, 1904. Alaska State Library, Case & Draper Collection, P39-0791.

far away in the wilderness, in which they live while they prepare and smoke their fish. They always have in their sight, though, preparing for the fall feast. They squirrel away for the feast the money they earn by working for white gold prospectors or in the canneries. When they come home to the villages, they buy many blankets and much cotton fabric, as well as food items for the feast. There is a great feast that they hold only once every twenty-fifth or fiftieth year. The richest in the whole clan gives away all his wealth, which consists of blankets. There was a chief in Sitka who held such a feast about twenty years ago. This chief had collected three thousand blankets and a lot of cotton fabric, which he gave away. And there were representatives there from other places who were the subjects of the great chief's generosity. They know nothing greater than to hold a potlatch-feast and give away all they can. The more they give, the higher stature the clan enjoys.

During the fall feast they want to make merry. When everything is ready, they gather in a large house, the different clans in different teams. The feast is divided into separate acts, such as the food feast, gift feast, weeping feast, dance feast, and magic feast. Everything bears the imprint of darkness and the thickest paganism. They like blankets and cotton fabric. The brighter the colors, the better, in their opinion.

The feast begins with the beating of drums. A large wooden chest serves as the bass drum. They paint themselves in the face, red, black, green, striped, and in totem characters. They buy sugar, rice, beans, syrup, and so on from the whites. From their own supplies, they have fish, birds, seal meat, oil, dried berries, roots, seaweed, and so on. They gather all the supplies together. Every family has a huge four- or five-gallon bowl. They place themselves in a rectangle and a team of young men hands out sugar, etc. And so they eat and sing. Thereafter a group of women, clad in richly embroidered clothing, comes in. Then they dance enthusiastically, while singing and howling, creating a deafening commotion. Everything begins at once and stops at once.

The next act consists of a large number of red, brown, striped, and plaid blankets being brought in to be given away. The blankets are ripped into long strips, eight or ten from every blanket, and they are given away by the owner, whose name is called out, so that everyone can hear and see how many valuable items are given away. Thereafter the bolts of fabric are brought in. Two men hold up the bolt and show how long it is and how much this or that person is giving away. The people talk about it and praise it. The fabric is then ripped off in pieces, a yard in length or less, and is given away in the same manner as the blankets.

At the feast, everyone receives food, fabric, and strips of blanket, only pieces of one or the other sort. Then the women quickly sew dresses, shirts, and other clothing from all these many pieces of different colors and types. The result is gaudy clothing. But the worse its appearance, the better they like it.

Other feast acts with dark deeds and of a terrible nature follow. One of these is the feast for the spirits of the dead. The shaman carries it out. They might weep all night long, beginning at once and ending at once. The whole group wails loudly. The names of the great men and women who have died and left them are announced. They believe that their spirits come to them during the days of the feast, so they want to honor them. They build a fire and cast blankets, pieces of fabric, food, etc. on it. They call out the names of those who have lived and died, in the belief that the deceased accept the offerings. In this way they preserve the memory and friendship, as well as the companionship, of the deceased.

VIII

SUNSET IN ALASKA

Sunset in the Nordic countries is magnificent, but a sunset in Alaska is spectacular. The sun, which during the day has been so lovely, descends at the horizon. It is as though the light gathers in flames, kissing everything farewell. The wild Indian as well as all life stops, and it feels wonderful to be alive. Every day has its morning, noon, evening, and sunset, but it is the latter that we intend to try to describe.

In many places in Alaska the sun never sets during the summer. The midnight sun and the sunlight remain all night long though the transition is like a gasp of light. Yes, it is light everywhere. I remember so well that I could read newspapers and letters in the middle of the night. We did that especially when the boat happened to arrive during the night. Then no one slept. Everyone wanted news and was happy to live in a land where the sun never set in darkness. Thus often I sat in my little cabin by the beach, looking out toward the heavens in the west, where the sun's beautiful drama took place. Heaven glowed in red, yellow, white, and blue. It is impossible to name all the colors that mingled there at the horizon. The most unfeeling person could not help but be overcome by the beauty and refraction of the light, as peacefully and beautifully the last flame died. *That* is a sunset!

THE NORTHERN LIGHTS

I have seen the northern lights since my childhood in Sweden. I have seen them in America, as well, but never so splendidly as I have seen them in Alaska. One sees them best on clear winter nights. They can be seen in the sky in high-arched bows from one end of the sky to the other. It is as though heaven's angels played in a sea of light. The light displays in various forms, in bows, in streaks, in rays; casting themselves about, the light bows twist, roll, and break apart. It moves back and forth, lighting the cold night so that it becomes light as day. Under the winter night, heaven is lit like a sea of light in motion. Like a sea aroused by a storm, these light flames glow. More than once I stood, until I was thoroughly chilled, gazing upward in awe and wonder. Even the Tlingit Indian is moved. Only an unfeeling person could stand unmoved before such scenery. I observed that after a great display of northern lights, either very beautiful weather or a very severe storm and foul weather would follow. The latter was the most common.

CHIEF GEORGE NAA-KAA-NEE

The Tlingit people have in past times had their leaders, of which chiefs were the foremost. One of these became my friend and was a great help to us missionaries in our work.[52] He and his wife are now dead. Many interesting events transpired during his lifetime, and I will relate some of them here.

Long before we established the mission station in Yakutat, it happened that George Naa-kaa-nee received a free journey down to Portland, Oregon. A couple of white gold seekers had come to Yakutat to find gold. They hired two Natives to assist them and they steered a canoe full of provisions to the tall mountains. Upon arriving there, they planned to go ashore and set up camp. The whites set out to gather firewood and left the Natives where they tied the boat, thinking that all was well. When they returned, the Indians had taken their weapons; they shot them dead on the spot, disposed of their bodies in the sea, and took everything they had. But there were consequences for the murderers. A United States warship set out from Sitka, Alaska, to capture them. They were questioned and confessed, after which they were taken aboard to be transported to the States to be hanged. The chief was taken along, to see what the whites did with murderers. They were hanged in Portland, Oregon. George now was to travel home to his people to tell them what had occurred, which he did. Through this experience the Natives developed a sense of the white man's power.[53]

George Naa-kaa-nee was a friend to the whites and especially to the missionaries. At the beginning of our efforts, he did not want to believe in Jesus. He said: "Who is this Jesus that I should believe in? We have our shaman (Ersh-t). He is just as strong." The chief was a tall man with rather sharp reasoning skills. He was a good shot, and he had killed many bears, wolves, and seals. We did him many favors. Missionary Henrikson repaired his rifle. My wife sewed dresses for his wife and taught her to bake bread.

Eventually George was moved and stood up during a meeting and said that he was convinced of the story of Jesus. He wanted himself, as well as his whole family and the whole clan, to believe in Jesus. He was thus baptized, along with his whole family, as during the apostles' time.

Another incident may have influenced him. We had brought to the station a number of cattle, among them a large and lusty bull. One day George had been in the forest to fetch wood and had drawn his canoe up on the beach, where he had laid his sweater-blanket. The bull, which was grazing on the beach nearby, came and began to chew it apart. George came to me crestfallen. My beast, he said, was no better than their dogs. "I have promised you to shoot dogs that do damage, and now I want a promise that you will shoot this beast," he said. "No, George," I said, "the animal has cost a lot of money. But I will compensate you with a new sweater." He appreciated this and gave his approval with a smile. And he received a warm sweater-blanket, and I thereby maintained his continued friendship.

I invited George Naa-kaa-nee and his family to dine at our table many times. It was always interesting to listen to him when he told of his peoples' achievements, struggles, and bravery in years past against wild animals, as well as the difficulties of heathendom and darkness. It was entertaining to have a Tlingit as a guest. There had to be much food, for it had to go far. They ate everything. What they could not eat, they stuffed in their pockets or wrapped in rags. I saw women take off their underskirts and put food or flour in them. They liked white peoples' food very much, and when it was available, it fortified them and lifted their spirits.

Chief George Naa-kaa-nee was an able and good hunter. He was known and loved by the adventurers who visited Yakutat, for he had hiked through the country in interior Alaska. He knew the way to the great glacier, and he knew the many and dangerous rivers and inlets. Many retained him. Among his people he was respected and loved. He carried our mission in his heart and gave us his sincere support. Many unscrupulous whites wanted to offer him strong spirits and seduce him. George often would lead and guide expeditions and canoes in treacherous waters and unknown areas. At dangerous landing places he was hired to bring them ashore in the midst of huge waves from the sea. George Naa-kaa-nee was always reliable in whatever task he undertook. But poor George Naa-kaa-nee, in his devotion to duty in finding food for his family, often set out toward the icebergs in the worst of winter to hunt seals. For the Indians also want to have a little fresh meat. One time he found himself by the huge icebergs in a fierce storm that overturned his canoe. He fell into the cold water and nearly drowned, but he struggled to land in his frozen clothing. This took place thirty miles from the village. He was without matches, for they had become wet. But he did not lose his senses. However frozen and starving he was, he struggled for all he was worth and found some sticks of wood, which he rubbed until they ignited. But the reader can imagine how much work and time it took to start a fire in this way. It saved his life, but the flesh on his fingers froze. It was moving to see him return home from this frightful hunt. But however much he suffered and was so terribly frozen, his countenance bore the mild expression that always characterized George. He told how in his need he had prayed to God for help and rescue, gazing up toward heaven and the star-filled sky. Now he thanked God for his rescue from distress. He was a hero, that chief.

THE THOUSAND-YEAR-OLD WOMAN

The Tlingit Indians generally grew very old, before they came in contact with whites, evil and seductive people and were infected by their diseases and learned their evil habits and sins. The whites' evil abominations, vileness, and infectious diseases ruined them. They therefore have quickly died out. Barely half remain of what they were thirty-five years ago.

On one occasion—it was in connection with a sick call—I came into a miserable and very poor house. Many elderly were here. A large fire burned in the middle of the earth floor, fish hung from the ceiling, and hard-smoked seal meat hung there on sticks. I took up a conversation with an elderly, wrinkled woman. I told her of God and Jesus. She was flexible, accommodating, and paid notice to what I said to her. I wanted to find out how old the woman was, so I posed the timid question: "Koon kaa se yu wa häe?" She responded: "Je shratsee kleck thosend tak" (I think I am a thousand years old). She was old, but not that old. She had heard that a thousand was a very high number and wanted to make an impression.

Most did not know how old they were. But after we began with the mission school and taught them to read and write, they kept track of how old they were. The above-mentioned woman became a Christian. The Lord saved several of these elderly.

Jemmey Sha-ooshle was an old man. It was said that he had once been a slave and had been taken in a battle between clans. Jemmey Sha-ooshle was a cheerful man, who rather early had turned to God and loved the whites and especially all the missionaries. He was short in height and could no longer hunt. His eyes were dim, but he could fish well and brought much fresh fish to us. He visited us often, late and early, and was always a bit of a jokester. He lived in a smokehouse. Here he dried his fish and cooked his food. He often prayed at our meetings. On one occasion we heard him in all innocence thank God for having arranged everything well. He thanked God who created the tidewaters, for when the tide was low, he could carry his clothing down and lay them on the ocean floor and fasten them to large stones, and in this way God washed his clothes and helped him, an old man, he said in his prayer.

These elderly have now crossed over the border and are home with God, a victory for the mission and for God's kingdom.

STRANDED ON AN ISLAND

The mission work among the Indians was conducted in practical ways. We sought to interest them in and teach them many useful things with an eye toward the future, for the benefit of the people. Many places in Alaska are suitable for cultivation, and many crops could be grown to advantage. It also was well-suited for raising cattle. We made an attempt at that and acquired a cow and a bull, and the people responded with much curiosity. Most of them had never seen cattle before, and thus they perceived them as bears or dangerous wild animals. When we brought them ashore, they ran about and shouted in fear. The boys climbed up in tall trees to see. At this time we had several schoolboys at the mission station, and when they heard that we were going to have these large beasts at the station, they came to us and said that they would have to leave the station if we were going to have "bears" there, for in that case they dared not stay. We comforted them by explaining that they were not dangerous and would harm no one. But these animals were wonders for them. Men and women stood for whole days and watched them eat the grass that grows so abundantly along the shores in southern Alaska, because the precipitation is so high.

It became a chore for us to acquire hay and feed for the long winter. We had heard of "silos" and aimed to try to preserve the fresh grass. Three years in a row we tried to develop the knowledge to store grass in silos cheaply and simply. The third year Governor John Brady visited us and saw our silo, and at that time the grass was remarkably good. He was so pleased with what we had accomplished that he took photographs of it and in his yearly report recommended such a silo to all of Alaska's people, describing how we had made it.[54] He said that we Swedish missionaries had done more than everyone else for Alaska's people, for we had taught them how to preserve the fresh grass. However, we also needed dry hay. We taught them to dry it in the Swedish way, that is, to drape it over poles to dry it. We do it the same way, regardless of how much rain falls.

On one occasion during winter I was to row in search of some of that dry hay several miles away. I started on the journey early in the morning in a fishing boat. I filled it full and guided the boat toward the mission station. I was thereby going to steer my boat through a narrow sound between an island and the mainland. The tidewater came in strongly here. It was impossible to row the boat through the current, so I walked ashore, pulling the boat forward, but suddenly the current took the boat and pulled it from me. I was now left alone on the island in the middle of ice-cold winter, without a coat or food. These two items lay in the boat that the current took and carried toward the other shore. It was a good thing that it was not carried with the current out to the wide-open sea. But what was I now to do in the cold and on this island? I yelled with all my might in case there was an Indian in the vicinity, but in vain. All I could hear was the ocean's roar and the screams of the wild birds. I gathered some boards, stumps, and twisted willow twigs and bound them all together. With this raft and a tree branch I tried to reach the mainland on the other side. But when I pulled out, I saw that it was not going to work without my ending up in the water. I abandoned the attempt and thought that I would be compelled to spend the whole night there; therefore I prepared for the worst. I pulled down a bunch of thick, soft moss that the large firs bear so abundantly in these regions. I had a few matches in my pocket, but no ax, so I could not get hold of anything flammable to make a fire. However, I asked God to help me. The time passed quickly. It was growing dark and the sun went down in the west and darkness began to envelop the island in its black veil. By this time the tidewater had gone out, so the "canal" that separated the island from the mainland was fairly shallow. Should I dare an attempt to wade over in the ice-cold water? I found myself as good a branch as I could find to steady myself and I plunged into the water. It was ice cold, the current fought against me, and the stones on the bottom were slippery, but I managed to come over to the mainland. I was elated and ran on the shore until I reached a gold seeker's cabin. A hermit lived there completely isolated with a cat, but he was not at home. I went into the cabin and put on warm clothing and left my wet clothes and ate the food I could find. I took a boat that was there and rowed out and got hold of my boat and steered it toward home.

At the mission station they were worried and wondered what could have happened. They had sent out some Indians in search of me. I met them on the way home. It goes without saying that they were glad to see me home again. I was now chilled to the bone and drank everything warm I could get hold of and therefore began to sweat profusely. The next day I was on my feet again and restored to health. I thanked God that He had brought me home and rescued me from imminent danger. Home had never been more dear to me, and it was He, who is called "the great rescuer," who helped and rescued me.

AN ADVENTURE AT THE HOT SPRINGS

It has now been nearly thirty years since I visited the hot springs near Sitka. We were a group of ten or twelve missionaries along with two Tlingit boys. Our craft was a fishing boat, and we had to row this boat in tail and head winds. Our journey went between the islets, rocks, and reefs. The land we saw was mountainous. All the mountains fell vertically into the sea. We saw many waterfalls rushing down from the heights at whirling speed. There was especially one fall that caught our attention. We had come so far on the

Albin and Agnes Johnson with their children Donald (born 1894) and Ruth (born 1897). Covenant Archives and Historical Library, North Park University, Chicago, Illinois.

journey that we glided in to the notorious Redoubt. In past times there was a Russian village here with a church and school. Everything was now abandoned, deserted and empty. The old dilapidated log houses bore witness of former work and life. Now everything was decaying and only one small log house remained, which formerly had been the pastor's residence. I had slept here one night together with a number of younger schoolboys and missionaries from Sitka's Presbyterian mission station. That time we had been there to fish salmon, and we had caught a great number. This time our goal was the hot springs. But to travel through such a beautiful place without seeing and admiring the beautiful landscape was impossible. Few places on earth are as strikingly beautiful as Redoubt. The bay, which winds its way there between the islets, is stunning. One of the islets is completely round like a beehive, high in the middle and slanting downward toward the beautiful shore. On this island, says their theology, women were created by ravens.[55] At the end of the bay was a large flat area with a beautiful lake in the background, from which a river flowed out to the sea. This channel bore witness to the Russians' great era in Alaska. Here they had had a saw powered by water. Here they fished and hunted. Here various kinds of fruit were cultivated and here they had cattle, etc. I could not help wondering: Why had they abandoned such a lovely place? Who can answer that? To this day, as far as I know, it is uninhabited. Here we saw peerless beauty. It surpassed anything anywhere. A wonderful waterfall plunged down from the top of the mountain. Up there, undoubtedly, was a lake, or perhaps ice masses gathered in a huge water tank from which an enormous body of water cast itself straight into the sea. The water was as clear as crystal. The waterfall was big enough to drive a mill or a factory. The wonderful aspect of the fall was that the water ran out as if from a ledge, plunging vertically into the sea without touching the mountainside, despite its falling from a terrific height. The mountainside was overgrown with spruce, cedars, and bushes, as well as flowers. The hum, the roar, the water spray in the sunlight was indescribable. Alaska is not yet fully discovered. This place is one of the undiscovered.

But we said farewell to the wonderful Redoubt. Our goal was the hot springs, and in the afternoon we were there. Far from land we saw steam rising from the hot springs over at the foot of the mountain. We landed and pulled the boat ashore. The group, with three or four women, hiked up to the cute small houses that Governor Brady built. Nearby, up by the foot of the mountain, were the springs. We made use of the houses and prepared to stay a week to hunt, fish, and bathe. The place and land were less inviting than Redoubt. There were nevertheless beautiful spruce forests and bushes. A row of peculiarly arranged pits was dug in the ground. When the Indians came to bathe, they lay in the warm sulfur water to restore their health. They had bathed there since time immemorial. The whites had erected a magnificent bathhouse there. By means of iron pipes they had tried to bring the water into the bathhouse, but the pipes were corroded by the sulfur. Therefore wooden gutters were used to lead this amazing water into the bathtub. One spring had boiling sulfur-rich water; the other had iron-rich lukewarm water. Both were brought in together into the bathtub. When one was going to bathe, one had to prepare the bathwater several hours before one stepped into the bathtub, for it took a long time before the water cooled.

I have never had a more pleasant outing than this, together with these particularly amiable missionaries. We read, bathed, sang, and conversed, fished and hunted and picked berries, and enjoyed the magnificent scenery. To be sure, Alaska has lovely experiences to offer.

IX

THE CENSUS IN ALASKA, YEAR 1900

"Uncle Sam" gave missionaries many official assignments during the time I was in Alaska. We served as postmaster and assisted explorers who were there to study the flora, fauna, and glaciers, as well as with mountaineering.

Completely unexpectedly I received a government appointment as census agent for a district in southern Alaska. This was exceedingly interesting work. I had an opportunity to see into both whites' and Indians' lives. To count the people and gather all the information in Yakutat took a couple of days. But I was directed to visit all the villages located in the vicinity, as well as along the great river Alsek, far beyond the high mountains. I therefore received permission to set out on a long journey. My company consisted of one white and one Indian. A village nearly one hundred miles from Yakutat named Dry Bay was our first destination. We traveled in a large Indian canoe. Traveling in Alaska is rather difficult inasmuch as there are few or no roads to travel. The Indians have lived in the country hundreds of years without building a single little road. Everything is wild and impassable as far as the land goes. Therefore, one must travel during summer by boat through the lakes and rivers and along the coastline.

With our craft we glided in complete silence through the beautiful bays, up and down the rivers, in winding streams through which the Indians had traveled since ancient times. We came to a difficult place called Antlind. Here there was a four-mile-wide sandy desert over which we had to carry or drag our canoe. We set up our tent on the wonderful plain. The ocean was on the one side and at the northern end of the plain, which was about twenty miles long, lay a glacier so large that one could not see over it. Apparently this desert was formed by the ice rivers from the icebergs, which float down and carry soil that is deposited, thereby forming land. I wondered how we would get the boat and our gear over the plain. But then I found an empty new barrel on the beach. I had the idea to make a trolley from it and began to cut a hole in both ends of it with my tallow knife, to make an axle. Thus we had a trolley, on which we placed the boat. The wind, fortunately, was a tailwind; therefore I set up a sail, and thus by this peculiar means of transport we moved forward over the desert. The wind helped us, but it nevertheless went slowly, for the load was heavy and the transport trolley poor. It took us the whole day to cross the plain.

Then we came to another river that in translation is called the Dangerous River. We set up camp here with the boat directly at the entrance of the tent. The next day we were up early and had loaded everything; then we pushed our boat over the river. The Indians fear it, because, they say, it has taken many lives. The current is very strong, and there are clay and sand banks here and there. Everything went well for us, but then we came upon yet another desert, nearly as broad, that we had to cross, and that meant repeating the same work. We encountered another difficulty, namely that the sand whirled about, and it was nearly impossible to travel forward. It took one day to cross this desert. We had now arrived near the coastline. The sandstorm increased more and more. We had to crawl into the tent and try to rest, but there was not much rest because of the swirling sand. Sand got in everything we had, and we could not find freshwater, for the seawater flowed up everywhere. We nearly died of thirst. The next day we loaded our boat and rowed several miles up a river before we found freshwater. If I have ever thanked God for water and really valued it, it was on this occasion.

We continued for another few days across rivers and lakes and streams under adventurous circumstances, and finally arrived at Dry Bay, where we set up our tent near a tributary to the large river Alsek. We stayed there for two days. There was an old Indian village that was very isolated there. It had only a few old-fashioned houses. We were very well received. I counted the people and found that 167 people lived in three houses. After I had counted them, I arranged a meeting and had the joy of gathering them around God's word. The shaman and the chief opened their homes and wished us welcome. I preached for them and invited them to Jesus. After the meeting it was moving to see many pray to God for mercy and salvation. This was the first time that this village had heard the good news of Jesus.

But how was I going to find my way into the country along the Alsek River? It would have taken all summer, and besides, I was not equipped. Instead I learned from these Indians how many lived in there, for they traveled there to hunt and fish.

Along this river are long stretches of undiscovered and nearly impassable land. The return journey went a little faster, but it was just as much work. We had become more accustomed to adventure, though. When we finally came home, we thanked God, who had been with us on the journey. My spouse had taken charge of the work at home and had held the gatherings. The people in the village had been very kind toward her and helped out with the meetings.

IMPLEMENTATION OF THE LAW IN ALASKA

Ever since Alaska was taken over by the United States, a stream of adventurers, gold seekers, hunters, traders, tourists, and explorers have traveled over the country. And here they have found a Goshen for their efforts.[56] In the mountains and on the beaches they have found gold. For hunters the land has been rich with game, and large corporations have earned millions on Alaska's salmon, which are the world's largest.

Not all who have come have been good people. Many were of low moral stature. Their influence was and is like the plague. Their goal was to profit from the ignorant savage. They have brought with them illnesses of the loathsome and corrupting sort, whereby death has snatched away thousands. Imagine how tuberculosis has ravaged the villages. When it first appeared, the magic men led the people to believe that the infected were possessed. For some time it appeared as though the Native people would die out entirely. They bled from a thousand wounds. Then also the influenza came to Alaska and snatched away a great number. There were villages where nearly everyone died. Crying children were found in the arms of their mothers, who lay cold and dead. It was so horrific that strong men shuddered at these scenes.

U.S. Revenue Cutter *Richard Rush* in Sitka harbor, 1880–1885. Thomas W. Benham photographs circa 1880–1890, Archives and Special Collections, Consortium Library, University of Alaska Anchorage, UAA-hmc-0069-b1.

If the people ever valued the missionaries, it was in these trying times. But they had to learn to pray and place themselves in God's hands. A large harvest has already been saved for the heavenly sanctuary.

An immoral lifestyle and the sale of strong drinks have been a strong hindrance to the mission's success in Alaska. The immoral whites want to live with no reins, and while we missionaries taught the Indians to believe in God and perform useful tasks, these seducers taught them fornication, gambling and drunkenness, dancing, etc. On one occasion when such spoilers carried on wildly and only laughed at us missionaries, I requested and received help from authorities in Sitka. The governor and a judge came up to Yakutat with a large warship.[57]

Our church was opened to accommodate them. All the whites who lived illegally with Indian women received their judgment of going to the priest to be married or going to prison. Many now came with their brides, and weddings were arranged in all haste. They came clad in their regular clothing. I made the ceremony short.

Now they tasted the law's hammer blow. One white rogue had to go to prison, inasmuch as he had sold liquor to the Indians. One poor man had become intoxicated and in his drunkenness had bitten off his wife's finger. He was fined. There was one Indian who bought a barrel of liquor from a smuggler and hid it on an island in the sea. He had planned to go there and drink, but the authorities caught wind of this. Charges were brought against him, and he was punished and imprisoned. Then he awakened and confessed the whole of his sin. He said: "Satan had been on top of me trying to crush me and plunge me into the abyss. Now I want to be saved and not drink the firewater any more, but rather believe in Jesus." He was an apostate, but was reformed. Another Native who lived in polygamy was taken to Skagway. He was sentenced to travel home and divorce his many wives and marry the first one he had taken. He had to bow to the law and thus came to me according to the judge's order. And when I, according to the ritual, asked: "Will you take this N.N. for your wife and love her in sickness and in health?" he responded, "That is a strange question, Johnson, since I have owned her as my wife for over seventeen years." I replied: "But now you must obey the judge and God." He therefore answered "yes" to the question.

A country must have laws and punishment for those who commit evil, for all the good laws are from God and have their roots in Him. Therefore in recent years several judicial districts have been established, along with commissioners here and there, as well as Indian police, who implement the law.

Several events in conjunction with alcoholic drinks could be cited. The white man who smuggles strong drinks to the heathen is guilty of an evil sin. There were great temptations for the Natives, even for the believing. They told me how strong the temptation was for them. One woman said that she felt as though she could offer everything she owned, even her little child, whom she loved so deeply, if she only could get hold of liquor. The Russians first taught the Natives to drink. Ever since, this deluge has flowed here to these poor people. It was first through the evangelical mission that they had their eyes opened and saw how it destroys them. One of our Christian women, before she was converted, was a strongly passionate drinker. We were to celebrate Christmas and were in a hurry, and right in the middle of the Christmas rush, she came to me and said: "Now, Johnson, it will soon be Christmas, and you'll have to promise me that I can drink a little, for at Christmastime shouldn't there be happiness?" I responded: "No, drinking is a great sin. God forbids it and the United States also forbids it." She said: "Really? Then I will obey you," and she kept her promise and remained faithful.

We missionaries constantly had to fight the liquor smuggling with tooth and nail to help the people. When the steamer from the States arrived in the villages in Alaska, there was always much excitement among Alaska's residents, who lived so isolated. On one occasion the big steamer was in the harbor, and all those who could do so met the steamer in canoes. Men, women, and children came. Much trade transpired, selling curiosities, skins, etc. A little cunning Japanese man, who stayed near Yakutat, learned to get hold of liquor and smuggle it out to the Tlingit. My spouse learned of it. And in a snap she set out in the company of Miss Jenny Olson, a missionary, to the Japanese man's house, in the style of Carrie Nation, to destroy the liquor that he had gotten and was going to trade. As they came into the cabin, they saw an Indian already there, likely in the act of acquiring liquor. Now my wife ordered the Japanese in a loud and commanding voice to turn over the liquor bottles and follow them to the mission station. He was frightened and followed, and at the mission station the liquor was locked up. Quite a commotion ensued among the thirsty drinkers. Every day the Japanese and others tried to persuade her by hook or by crook to release the merchandise, but no pleas helped in this regard. But the question was where could we get rid of the merchandise? It was spring, and my spouse and I were prepared to leave for the States. We had to resolve the business with the Japanese. He wanted to have the merchandise, but we were resolved that it was never to come into someone's hands so that any harm could come of it. Finally she paid the Japanese what he had paid. Then she took the bottles, and in the company of the Japanese and others, she broke them, so that the liquor and the pieces of glass flew. The Japanese trembled and bemoaned the loss, but we were happy, in the name of the Lord, for the victory over evil.

X

THE FRUITS OF THE MISSION WORK

The narrative written above shows many fruits. In the earliest days, one branch of the operation was to establish a children's home and hold school. Now the younger set can look forward to a brighter future. They are able to learn much of value, live better, clothe themselves better, have the opportunity to hear of God, and learn the whites' customs and traditions. Alaska therefore is continually developing for the better.

Now even railroads have been built. The biggest and longest goes from Seward to Fairbanks, about five hundred miles. It was the inauguration of this railroad that cost President Harding his life.[58] He was the only president who visited the country, but I hope he will not be the last.

In Alaska there are now several cities with all the modern facilities and improvements. The Alaska mission also seems to be a light bearer for Siberia's

Yakutat in 1904. Archives, University of Alaska Fairbanks, Orville George Herning Papers 1986-95-9.

poor people. I therefore cannot help praying to the Lord of the harvest that He will send the light there so that the many thousands of nomads, who are chained in the fetters of paganism, may receive the light and the Gospel. To bring the Gospel there was the original thought of our leading brothers in Sweden, when Karlson and Lydell traveled to Alaska. Has the time come yet? Will Brother Höijer be an inducement for us to bring the gospel there or will the door still be closed? The difficulties are great, but God lives, and if it goes according to His will, then the pagan doors must open, however much will be required of our dear Mission Organization here in America to oversee it, and however much work for the mission itself. For it will be interesting work, rewarding work, and productive for God's kingdom. Who would not want to be a part of such work?

What I have recorded in this book are dear memories. Farewell, Alaska! The time that I had the pleasure of working within your doors was interesting and educational. I learned to love the people and the country. I consider it grace that I was there in the earliest days. May we, on that great day, meet many who were won for God. How fun it was to sing and preach up there in Alaska! How moving it was to hear the Natives witness and pray to God in Alaska's language. What memories we missionaries carry with us! May the Lord bless the continuing work, and may our dear missionaries cooperate there so that even greater victories may be won! May your walls and palaces be tall, your doors wide, and God's work spread, that God's spirit may rest over the land of the north!

Notes

1. Västergötland was a historical province or *landskap* in southwestern Sweden.
2. Johnson's surname is not the same as his parents, because when he was born, Sweden still followed the tradition whereby the son of John received the last name Johnsson. Johan is the Swedish equivalent of John. At some point, Johnson, like many American immigrants, dropped the second *s*.
3. Henric Schartau was a pietistic Lutheran pastor who developed a systematic approach to the notion of salvation, which was grounded in scripture but influenced by Pietism (Olsson, *By One Spirit,* 60). Schartauanism was one of several "free-church" revival movements that challenged the established Lutheran Church of Sweden in the 1800s.
4. Folk school went through grade nine.
5. Jönköping is a city at the southern tip of Lake Vättern in historical Småland, a *landskap* in southern Sweden, just to the east of Västergötland. It was a center of much revival activity in the 1800s.
6. Ångermanland was a *landskap* in eastern Sweden well north of Stockholm. Norrland was the northernmost (of three) *landsdel* in Sweden and included nine *landskap*, one of which was Ångermanland. Ådal is a river valley in Ångermanland.
7. Kristinehamn lies in central Sweden, west of Stockholm. The Mission School in Kristinehamn was one of two in Sweden at the time. Initially it was a two-year school, but in 1888 it became a three-year school. In 1890 it was moved to Stockholm (Nordisk Familjebok, "Svenska Missionsförbundets Missionsskola").
8. Värmland is a *landskap* in middle Sweden that borders Norway on the west.
9. In Sweden at the time, if one moved from one parish to another, one had to report the migration to a parish official, who would record the vital information on a *flyttningsbevis* (transfer ticket) that would be presented to the parish official where the person moved. Because Johnson was leaving the country, no such "pass" was issued. His emigration would have been recorded at the port in Gothenburg, however (Roots Web, "Emigration: Tracing Their Tracks").
10. Apparently Johnson traveled first to England, as was typical at the time for Swedish emigrants, and then he boarded the SS *Alaska,* likely in Liverpool, and sailed from there to New York.
11. Johnson spelled it "Murier," but clearly he meant Muir Glacier, in Glacier Bay National Park, which is named after the naturalist John Muir.
12. This is a commonly recited saying that rhymes in Swedish: *Lycken kommer, lyckan går, den Gud älskar lyckan får.*

13. Johnson used in his text the term *vildarne*, which translates literally to "wild ones," the logical equivalent of savages. Though the term *savages* is offensive to twenty-first-century eyes and ears, it was used throughout the Western world to describe "uncivilized" or traditional peoples in various parts of the world, including indigenous Americans and members of African tribes. Johnson used the term eight times in the book. Much more often he used the terms *inföding* (Native) and *hedning* (heathen or pagan). I have been faithful to his use of these terms.
14. Explorer William Topham had written in 1889 of being annoyed by the "innumerable" dogs in Yakutat the year before (in Frederica de Laguna, *Under Mount Saint Elias,* 195).
15. Luke 19:40. As Jesus rode triumphantly into Jerusalem on what is now known as Palm Sunday, days before the crucifixion, he was greeted by throngs of his followers who sang his praises, as Satshrook did. Many of Jesus' devotees were society's outcasts, like Shatsrook. The Pharisees, feeling threatened by this open expression of adoration for Jesus, especially from the powerless, demanded that he quiet the crowd. Jesus' response, "if these become silent, the stones will cry out," meant that the voices of the downtrodden could not be silenced; if they were, other voices would cry out.
16. "Martha's concerns" refers to household tasks; this is a reference to Luke 10:40–42, wherein, during a visit by Jesus in their home, Martha was distracted by household duties, while Mary sat at the feet of Jesus and listened.
17. The *julotta* is an early morning (typically 7:00 a.m.) church service on Christmas in Sweden. On this morning in Yakutat the young people were caroling.
18. The village on Khantaak Island, at Port Mulgrave, west across Monti Bay from the mission house, had been established about 1880, because trading schooners had begun to stop there regularly (de Laguna, *Under Mount Saint Elias,* 319). In 1888 or 1889 the Tlingit began to move to the mainland to be close to the mission and the store, and by 1899 the village on Khantaak Island was abandoned, all residents having moved to the mainland (ibid., 321).
19. Stick Indians, also known as Tagish, are a group of northern Athabaskan Indians of northwest Canada and southeast Alaska.
20. According to Esther's grandson, Bertrand Adams, who writes under the pen names Kadashan and Naats'keek, the Johnsons treated Esther as a daughter. She was educated well and learned to play the piano, violin, and guitar. After she earned her high school diploma at the age of sixteen, Governor Brady hired her as a cook and housekeeper in the governor's mansion in Sitka. She worked there for four years, also entertaining his guests with her musical abilities. She married and moved back to Yakutat (Kadashan, *This Is Yakutat*).
21. I am unable to find reference to this verse in Swedish or in English.
22. During the 1840s in Sweden a phenomenon called "preaching sickness" emerged. Children or young people, usually, especially young women, would fall into trances, see visions of hell and the judgment, and exhort their listeners to repent. They were believed to be clairvoyant and had profound effects on those in their presence, sometimes bringing about transformations within whole communities through repentance, casting away of worldly possessions, taking of sobriety vows, and so on (Olsson, *By One Spirit,* 60–61). De Laguna (*Under Mount Saint Elias,* 723) uses the term *shouters* for what Swedes called *roparna*. I use the term *criers*, as Olsson and David Nyvall (*Swedish Covenanters*) did. Either is technically correct.

23. Just as the Bible makes numerous references to disciples and mission work using agricultural metaphors of sowing and reaping, Johnson's references to fruit, first sheaves, and so on reflect this concept of sowing the word of God and later reaping the fruits in souls won for Christ. As Hjalmar Sundquist wrote in his history of the Swedish Covenant, "The story of the Mission Covenanters is a story of sowing and reaping—a story of grains of wheat cast into the ground, germinating and growing, and in due season bringing forth their harvest" (Sundquist, "The Mission Covenanters," 19). He went on to clarify: "but after all God gave the increase" (ibid., 20).
24. Interestingly, when David Nyvall wrote of the criers in the context of the nineteenth-century revival era in Sweden, he suggested that the widespread depravity in Sweden gave rise to these calls to repentance: "It was an exceedingly coarse time, made worse because of the drink habit. Not infrequently the burden of guilt in the secrecy of many hearts found a voice that stirred whole communities in the so called 'Criers,' individuals who, while falling asleep, spoke words of warning and urged repentance, sometimes even pointing out individuals who were present and revealed secret crimes on their conscience, commanding them to return stolen goods to the right owner or otherwise making public confession of their sins" (Nyvall, *Swedish Covenanters*, 36).
25. Here where I have written "magic men" Johnson used the word *trollgubbarna*—the troll men or the magic men. At times he appears to have used the terms *schaman* and *trollgubbe* (singular) interchangeably. I have translated according to his use: *trollgubbe* as magic man and *schaman* as shaman.
26. *Missionären* ("The Missionary") was one of two weekly publications of the Swedish Evangelical Mission Covenant in America. David Nyvall was secretary of the executive board of the Swedish Evangelical Mission Covenant in America and the president of North Park College. Axel Mellander was also a member of the executive board as well as dean of the North Park Seminary and professor of theology.
27. Here ends David Nyvall's letter.
28. The term *siwash* referred to Native North Americans and today is deemed a derogatory term. In his Swedish narrative Johnson used this American term, which presumably was used in relating the story in Alaska.
29. *Tyee* is a term of Chinook Jargon or Pacific Northwest trade language that means leader, boss, or big chief.
30. A sea troll is a goblin.
31. De Laguna's informants of the 1950s offered a variety of traditional conceptions of the Spirit Above, some claiming there was just one, while others claimed there were many and that individuals had their own guardian spirits above. One informant explained that the Spirit Above did not create the world, but established the rules by which people were to live. Doing something wrong or violating the rules of nature could mean a person would not live long or would always have bad luck (de Laguna, *Under Mount Saint Elias,* 812). People's spirits or selves returned in newborn babies (ibid., 776). The Tlingit traditionally believed that people went to a variety of destinations after death, depending on how they died and whether they had been good or bad (ibid., 766). Some informants explained that there were several layers of heaven. Murderers, thieves, and other bad people went to "Dog Heaven" (ibid., 771).
32. The European name for the bird is diver. It is a member of the loon family.

33. For the first of Johnson's figures in this paragraph, he must have meant American square miles. His figure here and several below are off, however. According to Alaska's official website (www.alaska.gov) the state contains 586,000 square miles. It is one-fifth the size of the continental United States, and 488 times larger than Rhode Island. According to the state's Department of Natural Resources, Alaska contains approximately 375,000,000 acres of land (Alaska Department of Natural Resources, "Land Ownership in Alaska"). In 2006 Alaska's Coastal Management Program reported, using improved technology, that Alaska's coastline measures approximately 44,000 miles (Alaska Department of Natural Resources, "Alaska Coastal Management Program").
34. This is not a meaningful figure, as it does not indicate how deep the coal is. According to Pearson and Hermans' *Alaska in Maps*, Alaska has "as much as half of the nation's coal reserves—an estimated 5 trillion tons, with the energy equivalent of more than 1,000 Prudhoe Bays" (Roger W. Pearson and Marjorie Hermans, *Alaska in Maps*, 63).
35. The hymn is *How Great Thou Art;* I have used the standard American version of the hymn here, whereas Johnson's words are presumably the Swedish hymn in its original form. Translated quite literally, the poem, which Boberg set to a Swedish folk song, reads: Oh great God, when I view the world, That You have created with Your mighty Word, How You lead life's threads, And all creatures are satiated at Your table, Then the soul bursts into songs of praise, Oh great God, oh, great God."
36. According to Peakware World Mountain Encyclopedia ("Mt. Saint Elias") and other sources, Mount Saint Elias is 18,008 feet high.
37. It is unclear who this explorer was, but it may have been Israel Cook Russell, who led expeditions in 1890 and 1891 up Mount Saint Elias that failed to reach the top. The expeditions were sponsored by the U.S. Geological Survey and the National Geographic Society (de Laguna, *Under Mount Saint Elias,* 201–203).
38. Novorupta was the largest volcanic eruption of the twentieth century. Four years after the eruption when a National Geographic–sponsored expedition visited the area, so much smoke was still escaping from the thousands of steam vents in the thick layer of pumice and ash the volcano had spewed out that the expedition's leader, Robert Griggs, named the area the Valley of Ten Thousand Smokes (U.S. Geological Survey, "USGS Science for a Changing World"). Captain K. W. Perry of the *Manning* evacuated residents of Kodiak, the Alutiiq village of Katmai, and other villages. Remarkably, no one perished in the natural disaster. The residents of Katmai were resettled at a location named Perryville after Captain Perry (Gordon Pullar, "The Katmai Eruption").
39. De Laguna (*Under Mount Saint Elias,* 28) noted that "the earthquake of 1899... produced giant waves that destroyed forests up to 40 feet above sea level on the mainland north of Knight Island, washed away the graveyard on the southern tip of Khantaak Island, and resulted in changes of sea level, ranging from a subsidence of 7 feet at the western end of Phipps Peninsula to a maximum elevation of 46 feet on the west side of Disenchantment Bay."
40. Matthew 6:29.
41. Spanish explorer Alessandro Malaspina named the bay Disenchantment Bay in 1792, upon his discovery that the bay was not the entrance to the mythical "Strait of Anian" that Spanish explorer Lorenzo Ferrer Maldanado had reported in 1588 led to the long sought-after northwest passage from the Atlantic to the Pacific.

42. The garden of Hesperides is found in Greek mythology.
43. At this time it was often said that Mount Saint Elias was the tallest peak in North America.
44. Nabau, a town in the vicinity of Mount Nebo, is mentioned in a number of places in the Old Testament.
45. Nyvall's account ends here.
46. The governors' reports for the years 1911 and 1912 do not provide this information. It is possible that Johnson reported these data from a newspaper article.
47. Johnson appears to be referring to the Swedish west coast.
48. According to the Tongass National Forest Yakutat Ranger District's website, the highest temperature ever recorded at Yakutat was 87 degrees Fahrenheit (U.S. Forest Service, "Local Climate, Yakutat Ranger District").
49. Where I use "inch" Johnson used the term *tum*, or thumb, a Swedish measurement that refers to the width of a thumb; it is relatively equal to an inch. The annual precipitation averages about 146 inches, according to the Tongass National Forest Yakutat Ranger District's website. Extremes range from 85 inches to 250 inches (U.S. Forest Service, "Local Climate, Yakutat Ranger District").
50. Here Johnson clearly referred to plants that would be familiar to Swedes.
51. In 1805 the Yakutat Tlingit burned the Russian fort and killed all the Russian inhabitants of the fort, apparently some forty people. Accounts varied, but it appears that some Aleuts who were there, as well as the wife and children of the commander of the fort, may have survived (de Laguna, *Under Mount Saint Elias,* 173–175). U.S. Army Lt. W. R. Abercrombie, who explored the area in 1884, made the same assessment as Johnson regarding the Natives' acceptance of Christianity at Yakutat: "Christianity has made little or no advance among (the Yakutats)," he wrote. Though some wore crosses, they were worn as adornment, Abercrombie believed, rather than as religious tokens (cited in de Laguna, ibid., 186).
52. George Naa-kaa-nee was the second chief (de Laguna, *Under Mount Saint Elias,* 198). De Laguna (186) notes that Tlingit tribes always had more than one chief.
53. Isabel Shepard, who visited Yakutat in 1889 aboard the *Rush,* which was captained by her husband, related this incident as well. She reported that the murders had occurred in 1887, thus just before, rather than long before, the Covenant mission was established (Isabel S. Shepard, *Cruise of the U.S. Steamer "Rush"*).
54. Governor Brady wrote of the Yakutat mission's cattle and silo in his 1899 annual report (Alaska Governor, *Report of the Governor of Alaska to the Secretary of the Interior,* 1899, 18). He wrote enthusiastically of the prospects of agriculture, particularly in southeast Alaska, in his 1898 report: "In the neighborhood of Sitka, barley, oats, flax, red and white clover planted the last week in May all came to maturity, developing perfect seeds before the first frost... But grass beyond everything else promises to be the agricultural wealth of Alaska.... The native grasses are nutritious and grow luxuriantly.... One acre of ground in grass in Alaska for pasturage is worth several acres in a drier climate" (Alaska Governor, *Report of the Governor of Alaska to the Secretary of the Interior,* 1898, 203).
55. Johnson used the term *kråkor* (crows), referring to birds native to southern Sweden; however, this Tlingit story presumably referred to ravens.

56. Goshen was a district in ancient Egypt east of the Nile Delta where Israelites settled; it was thought to be the best land in Egypt, as there was both farm and grazing land there.
57. Johnson is referring to the 1901 incident recounted in the introduction to this translation, when Captain William Kilgore of the *Rush* brought Governor Brady and Commissioner Edward DeGroff from Sitka to Yakutat to investigate an extended episode of drunkenness and selling of alcohol.
58. President Warren Harding died, likely of a heart attack, while in San Francisco on his return journey from Alaska. He had visited numerous Alaska communities and driven the golden spike in the Alaska Railroad at a just-completed bridge at Nenana in the Interior.

Works Cited

Alaska Department of Natural Resources. "Alaska Coastal Management Program." Accessed 12 April 2012. Available from http://dnr.alaska.gov/coastal/acmp/Explore/Tourintro.html.

———. "Land Ownership in Alaska." Fact Sheet, Division of Mining, Land, and Water, March 2000. Accessed 12 April 2012. Available from http://dnr.alaska.gov/mlw/factsht/land_own.pdf.

Alaska Governor. *Report of the Governor of Alaska to the Secretary of the Interior.* Washington, D.C.: Government Printing Office, 1885.

———. *Report of the Governor of Alaska to the Secretary of the Interior.* Washington, D.C.: Government Printing Office, 1889.

———. *Report of the Governor of Alaska to the Secretary of the Interior.* Washington, D.C.: Government Printing Office, 1891.

———. *Report of the Governor of Alaska to the Secretary of the Interior.* Washington, D.C.: Government Printing Office, 1892.

———. *Report of the Governor of Alaska to the Secretary of the Interior.* Washington, D.C.: Government Printing Office, 1893.

———. *Report of the Governor of Alaska to the Secretary of the Interior.* Washington, D.C.: Government Printing Office, 1895.

———. *Report of the Governor of Alaska to the Secretary of the Interior.* Washington D.C.: Government Printing Office, 1897.

———. *Report of the Governor of Alaska to the Secretary of the Interior.* Washington, D.C.: Government Printing Office, 1898.

———. *Report of the Governor of Alaska to the Secretary of the Interior.* Washington, D.C.: Government Printing Office, 1899.

———. *Report of the Governor of Alaska to the Secretary of the Interior.* Washington, D.C.: Government Printing Office, 1900.

———. *Report of the Governor of Alaska to the Secretary of the Interior.* Washington, D.C.: Government Printing Office, 1901.

———. *Report of the Governor of Alaska to the Secretary of the Interior.* Washington, D.C.: Government Printing Office, 1904.

———. *Report of the Governor of Alaska to the Secretary of the Interior.* Washington, D.C.: Government Printing Office, 1905.

———. *Report of the Governor of Alaska to the Secretary of the Interior.* Washington, D.C.: Government Printing Office, 1911.

Almquist, L. Arden. *Covenant Missions in Alaska.* Chicago: Covenant Press, 1962.

Bowman, C. V. "About the Principles of the Mission Friends." In *Covenant Roots: Sources and Affirmations,* ed. Glenn P. Anderson. Chicago: Covenant Publications, 1999, 79–81 (first published in 1910 in the *Minneapolis Veckobladet*).

Brady, John. Letter to the Secretary of the Interior, 23 December 1905. General correspondence of the Alaska territorial governors, reel 14, Alaska and Polar Regions. Rasmuson Library, University of Alaska Fairbanks.

Burch, Ernest S., Jr. "The Inupiat and the Christianization of Arctic Alaska." *Etudes/Inuit/Studies* 18(1–2):81–108, 1994.

Calasanctius, Mary Joseph. *The Voice of Alaska: A Missioner's Memories.* Lachin, Quebec: Sisters of St. Anne Press, 1935.

Carlson, Leland. *An Alaskan Gold Mine: The Story of No. 9 Above.* Evanston, Ill.: Northwestern University Press, 1951.

Chapman, John Wight. *A Camp on the Yukon.* Cornwall-on-Hudson, N.Y.: Idlewild Press, 1948.

Cole, Terrence M. "Klondike Literature." *Columbia,* Summer 2008, 9–16.

Cole, Terrence M., and Elmer E. Rasmuson. *Banking on Alaska:* Vol. 1, *A History of NBA.* Anchorage: National Bank of Alaska, 2000.

de Laguna, Frederica. *Under Mount Saint Elias: The History and Culture of the Yakutat Tlingit.* Smithsonian Contributions to Anthropology, vol. 7. Washington, D.C.: Smithsonian Institution Press, 1972.

Dietz, Arthur Arnold. *Mad Rush for Gold in Frozen North.* Los Angeles: Times Mirror Printing and Binding House, 1914. Available from http://archive.org/stream/madrushforgoldin00dietuoft#page/n9/mode/2up.

Fienup-Riordan, Ann. *The Yup'ik Eskimos: As Described in the Travel Journals and Ethnographic Accounts of John and Edith Kilbuck 1885–1900.* Kingston, Ont.: Limestone Press, 1988.

Fortuine, Robert. *Chills and Fever: Health and Disease in the Early History of Alaska.* Fairbanks: University of Alaska Press, 1992.

Hinckley, Ted. "'We Are More Truly Heathen than the Natives': John G. Brady and the Assimilation of Alaska's Tlingit Indians." *Western Historical Quarterly,* January 1980, 37–55.

Jackson, Sheldon. Letter to Lyman E. Knapp, 20 September 1899. Appended to Alaska Governor, *Report of the Governor of Alaska to the Secretary of the Interior, 1889.* Washington, D.C.: Government Printing Office, 1889, 246–247.

Johnshoy, J. Walter. *Apaurak in Alaska: Social Pioneering Among the Eskimos.* Translated and compiled from the records of the Reverend T. L. Brevig, pioneer missionary to the Eskimos of Alaska, from 1894 to 1917. Philadelphia: Dorrance & Company, 1944.

Johnson, Albin. Ministerial Records. Record Series 6/1/2/1. Covenant Archives and Historical Library, North Park University, Chicago.

———. "Yakutat, 15 March 1905, Alaska-Missionen." In *Covenant Yearbook 1905.* North Park University Archives, Chicago.

———. "Missionsrapport från Yakutat, 15 April 1904, Missionen i Alaska." In *Covenant Yearbook 1904.* North Park University Archives, Chicago.

———. "Albin Johnsons missionsrapport från Yakutat, 1 February 1902, Missionen i Alaska." In *Covenant Yearbook 1902.* North Park University Archives, Chicago.

———. "Missionen i Yakutat, Alaska." In *Covenant Yearbook 1901.* North Park University Archives, Chicago.

———. "Missionen i Yakutat, Alaskamissionen." In *Covenant Yearbook 1900.* North Park University Archives, Chicago.

Kamenskii, Anatolii. *Tlingit Indians of Alaska.* Translated with an introduction and supplementary material by Sergei Kan. Volume 2 in the Rasmuson Library Historical Translation Series. Fairbanks: University of Alaska Press, 1985.

Kadashan. *This Is Yakutat.* Xlibris, 2005. Accessed 1 May 2012. Available from http://bookstore.xlibris.com/Author/Default.aspx?BookworksSId=SKU-0021912050.

Larson, Ernest B. "Our Alaska Mission." In *Covenant Memories: Golden Jubilee, Swedish Evangelical Mission Covenant, 1885–1935.* Chicago: Covenant Book Concern, 1935, 149–174.

Lazell, J. Arthur. *Alaskan Apostle: The Life Story of Sheldon Jackson.* New York: Harper & Brothers, 1960.

Mellander, Axel. "The Swedish Mission Friends in America." In *Covenant Roots: Sources and Affirmations,* ed. Glenn P. Anderson. Chicago: Covenant Publications, 1999.

Movius, Phyllis Demuth, ed. *When the Geese Come: The Journals of a Moravian Missionary, Ella Mae Ervin Romig, 1898–1905, Southwest Alaska.* Fairbanks: University of Alaska Press, 1997.

Nordisk Familjebok. "Svenska Missionsförbundets Missionsskola." *Uggleupplagan* 38. Supplement. Riksdagens bibliotek—Öyen. Tillägg, 655, Project Runeberg. Accessed 15 April 2012 from http://runeberg.org/nfcr/0364.html.

Nyvall, David. *The Swedish Covenanters: A History.* Chicago: Covenant Book Concern, 1930.

———. "The Swedish Evangelical Mission Covenant's Missions in Alaska." In *Report of the Commissioner of Education for 1895–96,* by Sheldon Jackson. Washington, D.C.: Government Printing Office, 1897. Accessed 4 March 2012. Available from http://www.archive.org/stream/reportoneducati00unkngoog/reportoneducati00unkngoog_djvu.txt.

Olsson, Karl A. *By One Spirit.* Chicago: Covenant Press, 1962.

Peakware World Mountain Encyclopedia. "Mt. Saint Elias." Accessed 12 April 2012. Available from http://www.peakware.com/peaks.html?pk=223.

Pearson, Roger W., and Marjorie Hermans. *Alaska in Maps: A Thematic Atlas.* Fairbanks: University of Alaska Press, 1998.

Pullar, Gordon. "The Katmai Eruption." Afognak Village History, Afognak Village Website, 2004. Accessed 7 April 2012. Available from http://www.afognak.org/education/history_chapter2.php.

Rasmuson, Edward A. Letter to the Reverend John Peterson, Secretary of the Mission Covenant Church of America, 13 October 1947. National Bank of Alaska Archives, Anchorage.

Rasmuson, Elmer E. *Banking on Alaska:* Vol. 2, *Elmer's Memoirs.* Anchorage: Rasmuson Foundation, 2000.

Roots Web. "Emigration: Tracing Their Tracks." Accessed 1 May 2012. Available from http://www.rootsweb.ancestry.com/~swewgw/Emigr/thEmiTrace.htm#Flyttningsbevis.

Shepard, Isabel S. *The Cruise of the U.S. Steamer "Rush" in Behring Sea Summer of 1889.* San Francisco: Bancroft Company, 1889. Accessed 1 June 2011 from http://www.archive.org/details/cihm_16145.

Strom, Charles Milton. *The Swedish Evangelical Mission Covenant Church of America: A Study of Immigrant Acculturation.* M.A. thesis. Davis: University of California Davis, 1990.

Stuck, Hudson. *Ten Thousand Miles with a Dog Sled: A Narrative of Winter Travel in Interior Alaska.* New York: Charles Scribner's Sons, 1916.

Sundquist, Hjalmar. "The Mission Covenanters: An Outline of History." In *Covenant Memories: Golden Jubilee, Swedish Evangelical Mission Covenant, 1885–1935.* Chicago: Covenant Book Concern, 1935, 17–104.

Svenska Missionsförbundet i Amerika (Swedish Mission Organization in America). *Alaska Förr och Nu: En Naturskildring, Kulturbild och Missionsberättelse, enlight muntliga och skriftliga meddelanden af missionärer (Alaska Then and Now: A Depiction of Nature, Culture and Missionary Accounts Based on Oral and Written Missionaries' Reports).* Chicago: P. G. Almberg & Company, 1897.

Swedish Evangelical Covenant in America. Minutes of the Ninth Annual Meeting, June 7–11, 1893. Record Series 15/0, "Translations." Covenant Archives and Historical Library, North Park University, Chicago.

———. Minutes of the Eighth Annual Meeting, September 15–19, 1892. Record Series 15/0, "Translations." Covenant Archives and Historical Library, North Park University, Chicago.

U.S. Forest Service. "Local Climate, Yakutat Ranger District." Tongass National Forest. Accessed 9 May 2012. Available from http://www.fs.fed.us/r10/tongass/districts/yakutat/area_info/local_climate.shtml.

U.S. Geological Survey. "USGS Science for a Changing World." Accessed 7 April 2012. Available from http://vulcan.wr.usgs.gov/Volcanoes/Alaska/description_1912_eruption_novarupta.html.

Updegraff, Harlan. Letter to Mrs. W. E. Young, 29 December 1909. Records of the Bureau of Indian Affairs, Alaska Division, General Correspondence 1908–1935. School Files, "Yakutat." Reel 27. Rasmuson Library, University of Alaska Fairbanks.

———. Letter to Reverend E. G. Hjerpe, Secretary, Swedish Evangelical Mission, 17 April 1909. School Files, "Yakutat." Reel 27. Rasmuson Library, University of Alaska Fairbanks.

Willard, Carrie M. *Carrie M. Willard Among the Tlingits: The Letters of 1881–1883.* Sitka: Mountain Meadow Press, 1995.

Znamenski, Andrei A. *Through Orthodox Eyes: Russian Missionary Narratives of Travels to the Dena'ina and Ahtna, 1850s–1930s.* Translated with an introduction by Andrei A. Znamenski. Volume 13 in the Rasmuson Library Historical Translation Series. Fairbanks: University of Alaska Press, 2003.

Index

Note: Italicized page numbers indicate photographs or illustrations.

F

G

H

I

J

K

L

M

S

T